Public Policy and Democracy

Dr. Manoj Sinha

Public Policy and Democracy

ISBN 978-93-83459-28-5

Author

Dr. Manoj Sinha
Associate Professor
Department of Political Science,
RamLal Anand College (Eve.)
University of Delhi

Published by

Bonfring
292/2, 5th Street Extension, Gandhipuram,
Coimbatore-641 012.
Tamilnadu, India.
E-mail: info@bonfring.org
Website: www.bonfring.org
Contact: 0422 3928700

Dr. Manoj Sinha
Associate Professor
Department of Political Science,
RamLal Anand College (Eve.)
University of Delhi

Dr. Manoj Sinha (b. 1965) obtained his M.A., M.Phil. and Ph.D. degrees in Political Science from the University of Delhi. He has been teaching Political Science and Public Administration at the undergraduate level at Ram Lal Anand (Eve.) College, University of Delhi since 1991 and has taught at the postgraduate level at Annamalai, Himachal and Delhi Universities since 1996.

His areas of specialization include Gandhian Thought, Political Theory and Environmental issues. He has also worked on Federalism in the Department of Political Science, University of California, Berkeley, U.S.A. He has presented a number of papers on Gandhian perspectives and environmental issues at various National and International Seminars and Conferences.

He is an active member of the Indian Society for Gandhian Studies and is associated with a number of academic organizations. Dr. Sinha has been a member of the Academic Council of the Delhi University and an Executive member of the Indian Institute of Public Administration (IIPA), New Delhi.

His academic work includes authorship of widely appreciated books like "Modernisation and Ecology: A Gandhian Perspective, National Book Organisation, New Delhi, 2004" and "Cooperative Federalism in India and the USA, National Book Organisation, New Delhi, 1998". Apart from these he has also edited a number of books like "Contemporary India, Orient Blackswan, New Delhi, 2012", "Gandhi Adhyayan, Orient Blackswan, New Delhi, 2010", "Prashashan Awam Lok Neeti, Orient Blackswan, New Delhi, 2010" and "Gandhi Adhyayan, Orient Longman, New Delhi, 2008". Besides he has also published a number of Chapters in various Books.

ACKNOWLEDGEMENT

I am overwhelmed with joy, and avail this opportunity, to express my deepest gratitude and sincere regards to people who in one way or the other have helped me throughout the year 2012 to complete my work successfully. The present work would not have come into existence without their altruistic contributions and efforts

The advice and encouragement I constantly receive from Prof. Sushma Yadav of IIPA for all the Academic endeavours I undertake cannot be properly expressed in the few sentences I am able to write here. Similarly my friend Dr Anil Dutta Mishra, himself an accomplished writer, invariably seems to know the ways out of the Academic maze I seem to tie myself into every time I undertake such a work. My senior and friend Dr Rajvir Sharma has also advised positively on this work throughout the project.

It gives me immense pleasure to express my deep sense of gratitude to my wife, Dr. Rosy Sinha for her timely advice and perennial encouragement throughout the course of my work.

I am also thankful to my children Piyush and Parag who were incessant pillars of support for me and created an atmosphere and gave me this golden opportunity to complete this book on "Public Policy and Democracy".

I also deeply acknowledge the unflinching support, motivation and constant encouragement of my late parents whose memory constantly helped me a lot in finalizing this project.

Dr. Manoj Sinha
Associate Professor
Department of Political Science
Ram Lal Anand College (Evening)
University of Delhi

PREFACE

The main objective of this book is to present a summary about two major topics: a) the process to formulate public policy decisions, and b) the principal methods to evaluate the impact and effects of a public policy. Both areas constitute core aspects of public policy analysis. Here I present their major characteristics followed by a brief discussion concerning their social implications and methodology.

The term government is consider here from a Weberian perspective, that it is the main social institution which gives national social units its coherence, representation, and a leading role. Its power is based either on a) tradition; or b) on charismatic features of leaders; or c) on a law and rationalistic basis. From this perspective, bureaucracy plays an important role in being a fundamental part of the public sphere, and its main "technostructural" column. Bureaucratic power is mainly evident in the stages of implementing and evaluating public policy. [1]

This book has eight main parts. At the beginning we are going to focus on the nature of public problems, how these problems are different from the private sector problems, and what are their main repercussions. A good understanding of this section is pertinent to the comprehension of the next chapters, and the main sections of this exposition.

The middle section is devoted to the discussion of the process to formulate public policies. Here it is important to keep in mind the influence from the real powers in society, namely the business sector, the international interest, and also some institutions, such as political organizations, special interest groups, churches, universities, and the armed forces. Complementary it is also important to be aware of the processes derived from the formal powers in society, namely national officials which are elected to represent society as a whole in a democratic nation.[2]

The final section will focus on the main methods to study the impact from public policy decisions. We do not expect to cover all the methods, but at least to present the fundamental methodologies and their main features. References respect to the implementation process for public policy making is presented at the end of this document. I will finish with a general presentation concerning the methodology for a public policy analysis situation. In this last part the objective is to synthesize the analytical aspects discussed in the other chapter of this book.

<table>
<tr><td>Unit</td><td align="center">Contents</td><td>Page No</td></tr>
</table>

Unit I

PUBLIC POLICY

1.1 INTRODUCTION

Individuals, organizations and the society at large are often faced with educational, socio-economic or political problems. In the face of such problems, decisions are taken to find solutions to the problems, so that they will not degenerate into uncontrollable stages which will make them difficult to solve. Public policies are made in order to solve a given problem affecting the masses in the society. A policy is, therefore, a decision as to what shall be done and how, where and when it shall be done.

A policy option made by an individual is known as private policy because it affects the individual alone and not other person. However, if a policy emanates from the public sector, such as from the institutions of the government and state created agencies, it is referred to as public policy. The term policy is often confused with decisions and rules. However, the term policy has a different meaning. Policy making may involve decision-making, but a decision may not constitute a policy. Decision-making, on the other hand, is the selection of one alternative from two or more possible alternatives. The Webster's Collegiate dictionary defines policy as a definite course of action selected from among alternatives and in the light of given conditions to guide and determine present and future decisions.

Policies are general directives or guiding principles issued by the legislature to direct a given course of action or the main line of action to be followed. A public policy is one formulated and implemented by the government for the use of the people.

There is lack of consensus over the meaning of public policy. **Thomas (1984:1)** defines public policy as whatever the government chooses to do or not to do. On the other hand, Ikelegbe (1996:4) defined public policy as government actions or course of actions or proposed actions or course of proposed actions directed at achieving certain goals. Similarly, **Leslie (1997)** views public policy as a course of action or inaction chosen by public authorities to address a given problem or a set of inter-related problems.

In any case, public policy refers to a proposed course of action, which the government intends to implement in response to a given problem or situation confronting it. This means that public policy can be regarded as general rules, regulations, guiding practices or actions in a particular activity or problem area. Public policies are usually formulated by the authorities in apolitical system such as the executives, the legislators, the judges and the administrators.

Generally speaking, public policy is defined as the authoritative decisions and actions of the government designed to solve a given problem or a chain of problems in a given society. The implication of this definition is that public policy is derived from constituted authority whose responsibility is to formulate policies through inputs of various policy actors.

Public policy making is a political activity which involves every active member of the political system. This is not to suggest that public policy-making is an affray for all-comers. To streamline the actors in the policy-making process, **James Anderson (1988)** distinguished between official and unofficial policy-makers. Those referred to as official policy-makers are those who possess legal authority to engage in the formulation of public policies. Public policy makers are authorized by the law to formulate, execute and evaluate public policies. In this category will include the legislators, executives, administrators, and judges.

Unofficial policy-makers refer to those who do not usually possess legal authority to make binding policy decisions, though they participate in the policy-making process and play important roles. The unofficial participants in the policy process include political parties, interest groups, and individual citizens.

Public policy usually involves the interaction of the civil society such as professional bodies, non-governmental organizations, and socio-cultural organizations that respond to the impact of policies.

Public policy is widely implemented in a state bureaucracy. This distinguishes public policy from private sector policies. The civil and public servants are, by their employment, responsible for executing public policies. This role is enhanced by their technical knowledge and experience in the service.

In addition, public policy involves the use of coercive agencies to ensure compliance. For instance, the government policy restricting the use of motorcycles on dual carriage roads within Abakaliki Metropolis is enforced by a task force. The task force was established mainly to achieve the policy objective. The role of such agencies is essential to avoid sabotage.

Allocation of adequate resources is essential for efficient implementation of public policies. This brings into focus the importance of budgetary allocations, which makes the implementation of public policies possible. Non-availability of resources can lead to ineffectiveness of public policies. As a matter of fact, any public policy that fails to receive adequate financial, material and personnel resources for its implementation can hardly be effective.

1.2. SCOPE OF PUBLIC POLICY

To have a proper understanding of public policy, it is necessary to understand its categories. A comprehensive understanding of the concept therefore, covers such areas, among others, as policy demands, policy decision, policy statements, policy outputs and policy outcome (Anderson, 1975).

POLICY DEMANDS

These are demands or claims made upon public officials by other actors (private or official) in the political system for action or inaction on some perceived problem. Such demands may take the form of insistence that government ought to "do something" to a proposal for specific action on the matter.

POLICY DECISIONS

These are decision made by public official that authorize or give direction and content to public policy actions. Examples are decisions to enact statutes issues executive orders or edicts, promulgate decrees, *et cetetra*.

POLICY STATEMENTS

Policy statements, according to **Anderson (1975)** are the formal expressions or articulations of public policy. They include legislative statue, decrees, presidential orders, administrative rules and court opinions, as well as indicating the intentions and goal of government, and how to realize tem, it is important to mention that policy statements are sometimes ambiguous and conflicting, they are sometimes conflicting in the sense that different and contradictory policy statements may be issued by different levels branches, or units of government.

POLICY OUTPUT

Policy statements, according to Anderson, are tangible manifestation of policies that is the things actually done in pursuance of policy decisions and statements. They are, therefore, what government does as distinguished from what it says it will do. Examples are health centers actually built, roads constructed, school built, industries built, et cetera. It is worth to not that policy outputs may sometimes differ from what policy statements indicate they should be.

POLICY OUTCOMES

These are the consequences for society (intended or unintended) that result from action or inaction by government. For example, the intended consequences of the current privatization policy currently being implemented in Nigeria are efficiency and high profit of the privatized firms, removal of government subsidies of public enterprises thereby saving billions of naira worth of public funds spent on them over the years, et cetera. But the unintended consequences are inflation and the consequent hardship for families due to low purchasing power of the naira. Again the capitalization policy and the merging of banks being currently implemented by the central bank of Nigeria might achieve the intended consequences of strengthening the banks thereby securing public funds, but, it has led to retrenchment of worker of banks which did not meet the deadline for capitalization as fixed by the central bank of Nigeria. These retrenched workers now join the mass of the unemployed in Nigeria.

1.3 TYPES OF PUBLIC POLICY

The categorization of public policy is a reflection of rests and idiosyncrasies of scholars of public policies. It equally centres on the ecology of the political system and focuses on the internal operation, issues and clientele or the purpose of this study, four categories are adopted for discussion:

a.   Distributive policy

b.   Redistributive policy

c.   Constituent policy

d.   Regulatory policy

DISTRIBUTIVE POLICY

This a brand of public policy that concerns itself with who gets what, when and how. It is the authoritative allocation of government revenue to a en section of the society or to a particular beneficiaries in a bid to respond to their needs. According to **Ikelegbe (1996: 16):**

These are policies which involve incremental dispersal, unit by unit, to different segments of the population, and to individuals and institutions.

The distributed values are in form of favours, spoils, benefits and patronage to some people or group of individuals and organizations. In distributive policy, the government stipulates the mode and method sharing the national or the common wealth **(Okereke, 1998:7).** As the most common form of policy, it uses general tax revenue to provide benefits to individuals or groups.

When federal, state or local government allocates specific grant for the purpose of solving public problems such actions are distributive policies. Some benefits are distributed without taking them away from other people, for example, free education: emergency services projects, provision of water or electricity. But this category of policy does not involve confrontation or dissent from beneficiaries. It rather brings the people closer to government and vice versa.

In the final analysis, distributive policies constitute the nerve- center of politics and governance. The policies decide what individuals or groups benefit or favour due to them in the society. As a response to the policy demand, the government comes up with patterns of impartial distribution of these resources to satisfy the citizens.

RE-DISTRIBUTIVE POLICY

Re-distributive policies involve transfer of resources of benefit from large groups or classes of people to another segment of the society. This is done through position of taxes on the advantages and used to assist the less privilege. There is gain and loss relationship among the beneficiaries of re-distributive policy. The benefits are *discriminatory* since the gain of one is the loss of the other. Class interests in this regard always characterize the distribution of resources, group or Class-related conflict and bargains. Such policies as Pay as You Earn (PAYE) tax system, Value Added Tax (VAT), welfare for disabled or impaired groups in the society, and educational policies are anchored on re-distributive principle. Most re-distributive policies are non-factual, especially at the stage of policy application since those not favoured could challenge and accuse government of deprivation and marginalization. In Nigeria, Education Tax Fund (ETF), Value Added (VAT), Petroleum Tax Fund (PTF) and so on are examples of redistributive Policies.

The government collects tax through these means and redirects the fund to other areas of need. In so, the gain and loss outcomes take place because while some group, pay, other groups benefit.

REGULATORY POLICY

The history of government has always been linked to the desire of mankind to be secure through law and order. This informs the introduction of regulatory measures. Thereafter, regulatory policy is a design to harmonize the actions of groups so as to protect the citizens. As **Egonmwan (1993:12)** puts it:

Regulatory *policies are those involving* setting *of standards and ivies to restrict the activities of sonic groups in the society in order to prevent undesired consequences of their action.*

The essence of regulatory policies is to prescribe code of conduct in human relationship, especially in the private sector relation enterprises. The policies include enactments to ensure that human relationship is conducted according to accepted norms, as prescribed by the policy. Regulatory policies have succeeded in changing the society characterized by brutality and nastiness to a society of tolerance and understanding.

The regulatory policies are always associated with punishment that results from breach or violation of rules or laws. In this case, sanction, coercion and incarceration are always applied as the instruments for realizing regulatory policies.

In Nigeria, regulatory instruments and institutions include Labour Law, Land Use and Allocation Act, Nigerian Drug Law Enforcement Agency; (NDLEA) Other regulatory agencies include National Board for Technical Education (NBTE) Independent National Electoral Commission (INEC), Joint Administration matriculation Board (JAMB), Nigerian Universities Commission (NUC) and so many others. As a regulatory policy aims **at** Providing protection and regulations of competition they are sometimes difficult to make and implement because of interest in bargain.

CONSTITUENT POLICIES

These are broad based policies that encompass all sectors of national life. They do not focus on Individuals for benefit or Punishment. They intended to favour the government and the public. Such policies as foreign policy and defence policies are examples. The special Concern is on legislation affecting the structure and function of government s as well as Policies governing their operations Nigeria, the following are some policy laws as Constituent Polices: The Unification Decree of 1966, the National Youth Service Corps Decree of 1973, the Universal Education policy of 1999 among others.

1.4 RELEVANCE OF STUDYING PUBLIC POLICY

There is an increasing upsurge of interest among political scientists, and public administration scholars and practitioners in the study of public policy- to the description, analysis and explanation of the causes and consequences of governmental activity. Since public policy affects the lives and well- being of citizens of any country, it becomes necessary and justifiable to study it in order to understand why governments do what they do or what they choose not to do; and to offer advice. **Dye (1981)** has advanced three reasons why the study of public policy it necessary.

SCIENTIFIC REASONS

Public policy can be studied in order to gain a greater knowledge about its origins, the processes by which it is developed, and its consequences for society. This in turn increases our comprehension of the political system and society generally.

PROFESSIONAL REASONS

The study of public policy promotes professionalism. As we noted earlier, this study of public policy enables us to know the causes and consequences of public policy. Once these are known, it becomes possible for us to prescribed and give professional advice. Such advice can be directed toward indicting either what policies can be directed toward indicating either what policies can be used to achieve particular goals, or what political and environmental factors are conducive to the development of a given policy.

POLITICAL REASONS

Public policy can be studied for "political purposes: to ensure that governments adopt the right or 'appropriate' policies to attain the "right" goals. In other words, the aim is to improve the quality of public policy in a desirable way, notwithstanding that substantial disagreement exists in society over what constitute "correct policies or the "right" goal or policy.

1.5 EVOLUTION OF PUBLIC POLICY ANALYSIS

Policy analysis is an important area in the study of public policy. As will be show in the subsequent discussions, it has moved from proposition to reality and has come to occupy a central place in official policy thinking the rapid acceptance of the legitimacy of policy analysis is one of the most remarkable developments in modern public affairs **(Ikelegbe, 1977).** So what is policy analysis?

Although the activities identified with policy analysis have been associated with public policy making throughout the history of governance, but the formal association of analysis with public decision-making is relatively recent. The theoretical roots of policy analysis can be remotely traced to an introductory essay by **Lasswell (1951:3)** where he expressed the view that:

A policy or orientation has been developing that cut across the existing specialization. The orientation is twofold. In part, it is directed toward the policy process, and in part toward the intelligence needs of policy. The first task, which is the development of a science of policy forming and execution, uses the methods of social and psychological inquiry. The second task, which is the improving of the content of the information, and the interpretations available to policy makers, typically goes outside the boundaries of social science and psychology.

But major impetus for the development of policy analysis was provided by **Dror (1967:197-203)** when he expressed the need for the development of a new professional skill called policy analysis to be concerned with the application of analytical skills to the solution of public problems. Dror made three major points:

1. Systems analysis with its classical emphasis on quantitative tools and an economic view of the world could be of only limited utility in government.

2. Policy analysis should combine proven methods of systems analysis with qualitative methods and full awareness of the special characteristics of political phenomena. And

3. Policy analysis should be institutionalized as a new professional role in government without pre-empting the functions of politicians and line executives.

In May 1974, the National Association of Schools of Public affairs and Administration (NASPAA), in issuing its first guidelines for members schools, identified policy analysis as one of five major subject areas which should be included in all public affairs programs. So policy analysis has over the years moved from proposition to reality, from a "fringe" idea to a central place in official public administration thinking. Since the 1970s, many institutes and departments have been established for public policy analysis in many countries of the world, particularly, in the United States and Canada. In Nigeria, for instance, the institute of policy studies has been established at the University of Calabar, and the University of Jos offers a Masters programme in Policy Analysis.

Unit II

THE NATURE OF PUBLIC POLICY PROBLEMS

2.1. DEFINITIONS

To understand many of the most important features of public problems, it is necessary to clarify terms in order to set the context of both the political and social conditions for public policy analysis. Several of the most commonly used terms are the following:

    a.   Events: Human and natural acts perceived to have social consequences.

    b.   Problems: Human needs, however identified, that cannot be met privately.

    c.   Issues: Controversial public problems.

    d.   Issue areas: Bundles of controversial public problems. [3]

Events naturally vary immensely in effect. Wars and natural disasters touch millions of lives. Inventions like the internal combustion engine have altered our life-style dramatically. A new family in the neighborhood, however, normally has only limited consequences.

Events may cause problems to emerge and set the conditions for resolving them. Whether this happens depends on how observers perceive events. Those directly affected by a zoning variance that permits construction of a new shopping center and apartment complex, for example, may identify specific needs created by this event; others affected may not identify any particular resulting needs. Still others, perhaps a group of environmentalists not directly affected, may identify a need for those living in the area and oppose the variance. Congruity in identifying and acting on needs is by no means guaranteed, and therefore many problems may result from the same event. Conflict among problem definitions creates an issue.[4]

2.2. PUBLIC AND PRIVATE PROBLEMS

If a problem can be resolved without making demands on the people that are not immediately affected, then it is private in nature. **John Dewey** explains it thus:

"We take then our point of departure from the objective fact that human acts have consequences upon others, that some of these consequences are perceived, and that their perception leads to subsequent effort to control action so as to secure some consequences and avoid others. Following this clew, we are led to remark that the consequences are of two kinds, those which affect the persons directly engaged in a transaction, and those which affect others beyond those immediately concerned. In this distinction, we find the germ of the distinction between the private and the public."[5]

A particular and essential feature of a public problem is the following: Human acts have consequences on others, and some of these are perceived to create needs to the extent that relief is sought. If the transaction to control consequences (regulating needs) is relatively restricted in effect, it is private. If the transaction has a broad effect, it is public. According to **Dewey**, "the public consists of all those who are affected by the indirect consequences of transactions to such an extent that it is deemed necessary to have those consequences systematically cared for."

People take actions or propose actions to control their environments: to meet their needs, to solve their problems. Sometimes these actions have consequences for others. When these consequences are perceived by others and considered to be significant enough to be controlled, we are facing a public problem. As **David G. Smith** explains: "That which intervenes between the perceived problem and the governmental outcome is a public, a group of affected parties-aroused, engaged in conjoint activity, growing conscious of itself, organizing and seeking to influence officials."[6]

In a more economic sense oriented, public problems, on the other hand, frequently involved the production and use of public goods, such as national defense, the national road system, and the general structure of the academic *pensa*. Conversely, private problems involved production and consumption of private goods. Public goods are goods -and in a broad sense services- that can be used by many people at the same time. Private goods have as a fundamental feature, the fact that it is not possible for two persons to use the same private good at the same time, i.e. personal cloths.[7]

2.3. POLITICAL FORCES WITHIN PUBLIC PROBLEMS

This concept of a public is important for these deliberations. Just as we have made a distinction between public and private problems, so too we can distinguish between public problems that have a supporting public and those public problems that do not. The first type of problem is characterized by a group of concerned and organized citizens who intend to get action; the second is acknowledged as a problem that cannot be solved privately, but it lacks organized and active support.

This distinction is critical for understanding the complex processes by which some problems reach government and others do not. The objective verification that a public problem exists (e.g., the many problems of the poor in most of the more developed nations) is no guarantee that a public will emerge to press for relief. As it is evident in many cases in the United States, "Public problems may lack a supporting public among those directly affected." Yet the government may act due to the demands of others. "Policy makers sometimes define problems for people who have not defined problems for themselves." This last condition can present several concrete opportunities for politicians especially during the political campaign and elections.[8]

Not only are problems private and public supported and non supported, this discussion shows that a whole bundle of issues may be associated with any one event-for example, the Arab oil embargo; the hostage crisis in Iran; the rapid growth, then decline, of the school population; the deregulation of the airlines. For this reason it is important to introduce the term issue area. What are often referred to as public problems-education, energy, mass transportation, housing-are in reality various conflicting demands for relieving several sets of needs among the persons within society. Complicating matters even more is the fact that needs and demands, and therefore conflicts and priorities, are constantly changing; issues therefore require almost continual definition and redefinition.[9]

2.4. POLITICAL SYSTEMS AND PROBLEM IDENTIFICATION

One can distinguish one political system from another by examining the characteristics of problem identification processes. In a democratic system problem identification is intended to be more subjective; in an authoritarian system it is intended to be more objective. In objectively defining problems an effort is made to employ scientific measures of the effects of events on people (this says nothing about the success of these measures, of course). [10]

There is little or no reliance on how the people interpret effects of events. Subjective processes, on the other hand, place a great deal of reliance on how those affected by an event interpret their needs. Elections and other representative processes presumably tap the public's subjective views. Both objective and subjective measures are, if fact, relied on by all political systems.

2.5. A LIST OF MAJOR ISSUE AREAS

One of the many advantages of an open society -in which a democratic political systems works, and civil society has an important and permanent influence on national issues-, is that evaluations of social progress come from a variety of sources. We do not have to await the announcement of a five-year plan to determine what should be done, like in the former soviet-socialist countries. We get frequent private and public assessments. [11]

Often presidents' national discourses and economic and budget messages, counter programs and messages from legislative branches, all constitute official evaluations of where we are and what we must do. In addition we in this kind of open societies, can see any number of critical and analytical reviews from private agencies and interest groups. In United States, for example, the Brooking Institution, an independent organization devoted to nonpartisan research, has for the past several years offered an analysis of the president's budget that has become a justly respected document. Groups like Common Cause, a citizen lobby, and the Ralph Nader Center for Study of Responsive Law are devoted to a kind of government watchdog function, and their reports naturally become source of information on public problems. [12]

While admittedly not altruistic in their endeavors, many national interest groups also performs similar functions as they search for policies, problems, and events that may affect their clienteles. Finally, some groups can provide data on what problems the general public judges to be important at any one time.

Taken together these various sources suggest a number of issue-area categories, that is, broad classifications of "bundles of controversial public problems." As a minimum these would include: [13]

Table 1: Issue-Areas for Public Policy Analysis

No.	Issue Area	Examples
1	Foreign	Relations with nations (individually and in alliances)
		Economic cooperation
2	Defense	Armed forces
		Security cooperation with other nations
		Arms special dispositions and treaties
3	Internal Affairs	Human resources, including health, education, welfare and job training
		Physical and natural resources
		Civil rights
		Social control and internal security
		Economic control
		Government organization
		Taxation
		Financial conditions
		Government expenditures

Source: Based on Stokey, E. *Public Policy Analysis*, Ob.Cit. p.10-12; and Jones, Ch. *Study of Public Policy Analysis*, Ob.Cit. p. 43.

National budgets in different nations reflect one catalog of needs and how those needs are interpreted as priorities. However, the accelerated growth of certain budget items, combined with a stagnating economy, has reduced the capacity of governments to respond to new problems. Some people, including many in the Reagan administration in United States, conclude that the biggest problem of all is the rejuvenation of the economy, and that can occur only with a reduction in government spending and influence -neoliberal social and economic perspective-.

Others doubt that this solution will work and call for increased government control of the economy -Keynesian, and Neokeynesian option-. It is apparent that the two groups are in agreement on one point at least: those certain major problems are not being solved by governments. Of both sides the budget is not the best inventory of major issue areas, a conclusion that has placed the budget front and center in the national policy-making system.[14]

2.6. ISSUES AND EVENTS

What events have created the needs leading to major national issues? Again the discussion must be conducted at a general level and must be designed primarily to explain contemporary trends. According to **Charles O. Jones**, there are five broad categories of events influential in shaping issues: events of discovery, development, communication, conflict, and control. Broadly speaking, these events constitute what John Dewey calls the "human acts" that "have consequences upon others." They are the starting points for tracing the policy process for any one issue. [15]

Unit III

THEORETICAL APPROACHES TO PUBLIC POLICY STUDY

Over the years, a variety of theoretical approaches have been developed by political scientists and policy analysts to assist their study and analysis of public policy. Although most of these approaches have not been developed specifically for the analysis of policy formation, they can readily be converted to that purpose. It is important to note that the choice of any approach by a particular analyst depends on his or her inclination, ideological outlook and/or training. It may also depend on the nature of the policy under discussion or the level of analysis whether it is at the level of the state, national or international **(Abdusalumi, 1988:3)** Equally worthy of note is that these approaches are useful in. and to the extent, that they direct our attention to important political phenomena. help clarify and simplify our thinking, and suggest possible explanations for public policy. What follows is a discussion of some of the approaches.

INSTITUTION MODEL

Perhaps the oldest approach to the study of public policy, the institutional approach, focuses upon the formal institutions of government (e.g. legislature, executive, court, political parties, bureaus, departments et cetera), describing their structures, organization, duties and expected functions, with little attention paid to the institutional characteristics of governmental policies **(Abdusalami, 1998:3);** as well as the linkages among these institutions. Also the behavioural connections between a department and the public policy emanating from it are of scant concern. Yet, the fact remains that an institution is a regularized pattern of human behaviour that persist over time (some people mistakenly equate institutions with the physical structures in which they exist). It is their differing sets of behavioural patterns that really distinguish courts from legislatures, from administrative agencies, and so on. These regularized pattern of behaviour which we often call rules, structures and the like, can affect decision-making and the content of public policy **(Anderson, *1975)***

In summary, the institutional approach conceives public policy as often initiated, formed, decided and implemented by government institutions. Therefore, an understanding of how these institutions work is necessary before the public policy making process can be fully analyzed. With the evolution and onrush of the "behavioural revolution" in political science, institutional studies of the policy process became unpopular among scholars who preferred the group, systems, and elite/mass models, in about that order of emphasis **(Henry, *1995* :296).**

THE ELITE MODEL

The elite model regards public policy as the values and preferences of a governing elite. In other words, public policy is the product of the elites, reflecting their values and serving their ends, one of which may be a desire to provide for the welfare of the masses. As **Henry** *(1995:295)* succinctly puts it; the elite/mass model contends that a policy making/policy executing elite is able to act in an environment characterized by apathy and information distortion and thereby governs a largely passive mass. Policy flows downward from the elite to the mass. Society is divided according to those who have power and those who do not. Elites share common values that differentiate them from the mass, and prevailing public policies reflect elite values, which may be summed up as: Preserve the status quo.

Using this approach, public policy analysis is largely an exercise primarily aimed at identifying which elite group(s) is or are benefiting from a particular public policy. A major defect of the elite theory is that it assumes the existence of a highly structured and stratified society, and by implication, elite values and identity. But as **Abdulsalami (1998:4)** rightly points out "In structurally diffused or "undefracted" societies, elite formation and, therefore, elite values and identity, are relatively undeveloped". In the particular case of Nigeria, ethnic and religious values rather than elite interests often influence elite preference, when certain policy issues are under consideration **(Abdulsalami, 1998:4).** There have been instances when the elite identified more with the aspirations of the masses of their ethnic areas or religious groupings than with the aspirations of their fellow elite

THE GROUP MODEL

According to this model, public policy is the product of group struggle. This approach posits that individuals are important only when they act as a part of or on behalf of group interests **(Dye, 1981:5)**. It conceives society as a mosaic of numerous interest groups, with cross-cutting membership. A group is made up of individuals that may, on the basis of shared attitudes or interests, make claims upon other groups in society. The group approach sees interaction and struggle among groups as the central fact of political life. The policy makers act as referees, arranging a compromise among competing interests. The group approach contends that public policy usually reflect the interests of dominant group(s). As groups gain and lose power and influence, public policy will be altered in favour of the interests of gaining influence against the interest of those loosing influence.

The group approach has been criticized for overstating importance of groups and for neglecting or understating 11 independent and creative roles that public officials play in policy process. Critics contend that many groups have generated by public policy, and that public officials may acquire stake in particular programs or policies and as a result act as I interest group in support of their continuance.

POLITICAL SYSTEMS THEORY OR MODEL

The political system theory is most closely associated with the work of **David Easton (1953).** According to this model, public policy is the response of the political system to demands arising from its environment. The political system as defined by E composed of those identifiable and interrelated institutions a activities in a society that make authoritative decisions allocation of values) that are binding on society. The environment consists of all those socio-cultural, economic, and political Conditions or factors within and outside the boundaries of the political system which shape the political process, and whose activities are influenced by the political system.

The political system receives inputs from the environment. Inputs consist of demands and supports. Demands are the claims made by individuals and groups on the political system for action to satisfy their interests. Support is rendered when groups and individuals abide by the rules or laws of the country, pay their taxes, and accept the decisions and actions of the authoritative political system made in response to demands. These authoritative allocations of values constitute public policy. The concept of feedback indicates that the political system receives information about the policy outcomes.

The political systems theory has certain limitations. First, it does not explain the origin of public policies, nor is it concerned with how decisions are made and policies developed within the political system. Again, it is not concerned with evaluation of past and present policies. Nonetheless, systems theory is a useful aid in organizing our inquiry into policy formation. Systems theory draws our attention to the influence of environmental inputs on the content of public policy.

CLASS THEORY OR MODEL

The class theory is most closely associated with the work of Marx and **Engels (1971:35).** The main proposition of the class theory is that public policies in a capitalist society reflect the values and interests of the dominant and ruling class. It states that capitalist societies are characterized by the presence of classes that have opposing values and interests. According to Lenin **(Quoted in Afanasyer, 1980):**

....Classes are *large groups of people differing from each other by the place they occupy in a historically determined system of social production, by their relation (in most cases fixed and formulated in law) to the means of production, by their role in social organizations of labour, and consequently, by the dimensions of the share of social wealth of which they dispose and the mode of acquiring it.*

The class theory argues that the mode of production and distribution in every society defines the character of the society. Thus, the class to which an individual belongs could be identified on the basis of his role in the social organization of labour, and his position to the means of production. Two broad classes have been identified by the class theory - the bourgeoisie and the proletariat. The bourgeoisie are the owners of the means of production, while the proletariat is the working class, whose labour is often exploited by the bourgeoisie. According to the class theory, conflict between these two classes is inherent in the capitalist society. According to Marx (Quoted in **Afanasyer, 1980:239**), "the history of class struggle - freemen and slave, patrician and plebeian, lord and serf, guild master and journey men, in a word, oppressor and oppressed, stood in constant opposition to one another". These conflicts often arise due to resistance of the proletariat to exploitation by the bourgeoisie.

The class theory argues that the bourgeoisie due to their economic power also control political power and use it to protect their socio-economic interests. This is often reflected in the type of policies they make. Thus, public policies often reflect the interests of the bourgeoisie. On the other hand, the proletariats attempt to influence public policies to their advantage through industrial conflict, such as strikes, work to rule, *etcetera.*

Unit IV

THE POLICY MAKING PROCESS

4.1. GENERAL FEATURES

A common dictionary definition of process is "a series of actions or operations definitely conducting to an end." Obviously process is associated with all forms of social behavior. Political scientists traditionally have been interested in institutional processed, that is, those "series of actions or operations" associated with legislatures, executives, bureaucracies, courts, political parties, and other political institutions. Many, if not most, political science courses focus on these processes: what they are, how they work, what they produce, and how they connect. Generalizations are developed about such processes as budget making, administrative rule making, congressional voting, priority setting, making appointments, reorganization, and committee decision making. More often than not, these generalizations cut across substantive issues. [16]

Focusing on group processes is also popular. In this approach it is assumed that groups are absolutely crucial in political decision making. One studies the role of interest groups but also looks for groups within political institutions. The latter groups may not always coincide with the organizational framework of the institution. [17]

The focus here is on public problems and how they are acted on in government. It is assumed that problems themselves help to shape the structure and organization of government, and that often cross-institutional and intergovernmental connections will emerge to treat these problems. Generalizations are developed about issues or issue areas as well as the activities associated with resolving them.[18]

4.2. CONCEPTUAL APPROACHES TO STUDY THE METHODOLOGY OF POLICY PROCESS

There are several conceptual process approaches to study policy making processes. They differ in terms of the focus of analysis and the nature of the generalizations. Examples of the more frequently used approaches are: a) focus on real social powers and institutions; b) formal elected officials as primary axis of representations; c) dynamics of different and relevant groups of pressure; d) historical social conditions and trend of political needs; and e) the external and internal political and economic conditions as social domestic factors. [19]

None of them is one more legitimate than the others; rather, each contributes to a fuller understanding of the others. Each is an effort to describe and analyze reality: for example, committees as institutional groups are real; interactions among outside formal groups are real; public problems are very real. Finally, each emphasis may reveal an aspect of the political or decision-making system that is obscured by the others.

These conceptual approaches need to deal with the concrete conditions in which a particular policy making process is carried out. For example, they must take into account who participates and interacts with whom in a particular matter. It may well be, for example, that not all members of a congressional committee participate in exploring solutions to a problem, whereas lobbyists, bureaucrats, and private consultants do. The student of group processes attempts to identify this cross-institutional participation and generalize about its nature. Various elite theories propose that decisions are actually make by small groups that may or may not communicate with their publics. In this view the group process is really an elite process. [20]

Some people are primarily interested in the substance of issues; that is, in the nature of the problems and how they can be solved. For example, they want to understand the essential elements of inflation, unemployment, or trade imbalances in order to identify alternative courses of action for solving these problems. Their expertise is related to these substantive issues, for example, as labor, economic, education, or trade specialists.

Many political scientists are more interested in process than substance. For them substance (e.g. inflation and actions to curb it) is merely a way to study process. Their expertise develops out of knowledge about the organization, routines, and decisions of government and other public agencies. [21]

4.3. DEFINING POLICY

Those studying the policy process do not have the advantage of a common reference. A definition is required to determine what to look for in "policy". The definition I favor is offered by Heinz Eulau and Kenneth Prewitt: "Policy is defined as a "standing decision" characterized by behavioral consistency and repetitiveness on the part of both those who make it and those who abide by it. [22]

This definition leaves us with the problems of determining how long a decision must stand, what constitutes behavioral consistency and repetitiveness, and who actually constitutes the population of policy makers and policy abiders, but it does identify some of the components of public policy.

Here then are two broad uses of the term policy: one as a word substitute or shorthand where common understanding is assumed; another as a set of characteristics to be specified and then identified through research. Clearly the second is more applicable to the present objective. For the purpose here is to encourage study of public policy and how it is made. We do not plan to conduct research on policy questions as such. The plan is rather to provide a basis for understanding the "behavioral consistency and repetitiveness" associated with efforts in and through government to resolve public problems. Used in this way, policy is a highly dynamic term.

As Eulau and Prewitt point out, "What the observer sees when he identifies policy at any one point in time is at most a stage or phase in a sequence of events that constitute policy development."[23] To put it another way, we freeze the action for purposes of analysis. Whatever we learn must be specified in terms of the questions we seek to answer, the time frame within which our research is conducted, and the institutional units being studied.

Therefore any reference to "defense policy," "farm policy," or "social security policy" should lead us to ask, What do you mean by that? Are you speaking of national goals? Current statutes? Recent decisions? Or are you characterizing certain behavioral consistencies by decision makers? The point of asking these questions is not to enforce one particular definition of the term policy, but rather to clarify meanings and thereby improve understanding.

One important observation is that, **Eulau and Prewitt** also observe that "policy is distinguished from policy goals, policy intentions, and policy choices."[24] What this suggests is that it is helpful to distinguish the several components of public policy. For example:

a. Intentions: The true purposes of an action

b. Goals: The stated ends to be achieved

c. Plans or proposals: Specified means for achieving the goals

d. Programs: Authorized means for achieving goals

e. Decisions or choices: Specific actions taken to set goals, develop plans, implement and evaluate programs.

f. Effects: The measurable impacts of programs (intended and unintended; primary and secondary)

One can reasonably use the term policy as an adjective with each of these components, but it does become somewhat confusing if the term is used interchangeably with all of them. We should also note the more legal terms associated with public policy making: legislation, laws, statutes, executive orders, regulations, legal opinions. these too are often called policy. For our purposes, however, they are simply the formal ingredients or legal expressions of programs and decisions. [25]

4.4. A POLICY PROCESS FRAMEWORK

From its origins in the 1950s, the fi eld of policy analysis has been tightly connected with a perspective that considers the policy process as evolving through a sequence of discrete stages or phases. The policy cycle framework or perspective has served as a basic template that allows to systematize and compare the diverse debates, approaches, and models in the field and to assess the individual contribution of the respective approaches to the discipline. At the same time, the framework has regularly been criticized in terms of its theoretical construction as well as in terms of its empirical validity. We are therefore confronted with an almost paradoxical situation: on the one hand of the policy research continues to rely on the stages or cycle perspective or is linked to one of its stages and research questions. On the other hand, the very concept of the stages perspective has become discredited by a variety of criticisms, including attacks on the theoretical status of the policy cycle as a *framework*, *model* or *heuristic* (we use the terms *framework* and *perspective* interchangeably, but return to a discussion of this issue in this chapter's conclusion). This chapter seeks to assess the limitations and utility of the policy cycle perspective by surveying the literature that analyses particular stages or phases of the policy cycle. Following an initial account of the development of the policy cycle framework, the chapter offers an overview of the different stages or phases of the policy process, highlighting analytical perspectives and major research results. Then we turn to the burgeoning critique of the policy cycle framework in the wider policy research literature. The chapter concludes with a brief overall assessment of the framework, considering, in particular, its status as an analytical tool for public policy research.

THE POLICY CYCLE—A SIMPLIFIED MODEL OF THE POLICY PROCESS

The idea of modeling the policy process in terms of stages was fi rst put forward by **Lasswell**. As part of his attempt to establish a multidisciplinary and prescriptive policy science, **Lasswell** introduced (in 1956) a model of the policy process comprised of seven stages: intelligence, promotion, prescription, invocation, application, termination, and appraisal. While this sequence of stages has been contested (in particular that termination comes before appraisal), the model itself has been highly successful as a basic framework for the fi eld of policy studies and became the starting point of a variety of typologies of the policy process. Based on the growth of the fi eld of policy studies during the 1960s and 1970s, the stages models served the basic need to organize and systemize a growing body of literature and research. Subsequently, a number of different variations of the stages typology have been put forward, usually offering further differentiations of (sub-)stages. The versions developed by **Brewer and deLeon (1983), May and Wildavsky (1978), Anderson (1975), and Jenkins (1978)** are among the most widely adopted ones. Today, the differentiation between *agenda-setting*, *policy formulation*, *decision making*, *implementation*, and *evaluation* (eventually leading to termination) has become the conventional way to describe the chronology of a policy process. Arguably, Lasswell's understanding of the model of the policy process was more prescriptive and normative rather than descriptive and analytical. His linear sequence of the different stages had been designed like a problem-solving model and accords with other prescriptive rational models of planning and decision-making developed in organization theory and public administration. While empirical studies of decision-making and planning in organizations, known as the behavioral theory of decision making (**Simon 1947**), have repeatedly pointed out that real world decision-making usually does not follow this sequence of discrete stages, the stages perspective still counts as an ideal-type of rational planning and decision-making. According to such a rational model, any decision- making should be based on a comprehensive analysis of problems and goals, followed by an inclusive collection and analysis of information and a search for the best alternative to achieve these goals. This includes the analysis of costs and benefits of the different options and the final selection of the course of action. Measures have to be carried out (implemented) and results appraised against the objectives and adjusted if needed. One of the major reasons of the success and durability of the stages typology is therefore its appeal as a normative model for ideal-type, rational, evidence-based policy making. In addition, the notion is congruent with a basic democratic understanding of elected politicians taking decisions which are then carried out by a neutral public service. The rational model therefore also shows some tacit concurrence with the traditional dichotomy of politics and administration, which was so powerful in public administration theory until after World War II. Lasswell was, of course, highly critical of this politics/administration dichotomy, so his stages perspective moves beyond the formal analysis of single institutions that dominated the field of traditional public administration research by focusing on the contributions and interaction of different actors and institutions in the policy process. Furthermore, the stages perspective helped to overcome the bias of political science on the input-side (political behavior, attitudes, interest organizations) of the political system. Framing the political process as a continuous process of policy-making allowed to assess the cumulative effects of the various actors, forces, and institutions that interact in the policy process and therefore shape its outcome(s). In particular, the contribution of administrative and bureaucratic factors across the various stages of the policy process provided an innovative analytical perspective compared to the traditional analysis of formal structures.

Still, the stages of policy-making were originally conceived as evolving in a chronological order—first, problems are defined and put on the agenda, next policies are developed, adopted and implemented; and, finally these policies will be assessed against their effectiveness and efficiency and either terminated or restarted. Combined with Easton's input-output model this stages perspective was then transformed into a cyclical model, the so-called policy cycle. The cyclical perspective emphasizes feed-back (loop) processes between outputs and inputs of policy-making, leading to the continual perpetuation of the policy process. Outputs of policy processes at t1 have an impact on the wider society and will be transformed into an input (demands and support) to a succeeding policy process at t2. The integration of Easton's input-output model also contributed to the further differentiation of the policy process. Instead of ending with the decision to adopt a particular course of action, the focus was extended to cover the implementation of policies and, in particular, the reaction of the affected target group (impact) and the wider effects of the policy within the respective social sector (outcome). Also, the tendency of policies to create unintended consequences or side-effects became apparent through this policy process perspective. While the policy cycle framework takes into account the feedback between different elements of the policy process (and therefore draws a more realistic picture of the policy process than earlier stages models), it still presents a simplified and ideal-type model of the policy process, as most of its proponents will readily admit. Under real-world conditions, policies are, e.g., more frequently *not* the subject of comprehensive evaluations that lead to either termination or reformulation of a policy. Policy processes rarely feature clear-cut beginnings and endings. At the same time, policies have always been constantly reviewed, controlled, modified, and sometimes even terminated; policies are perpetually reformulated, implemented, evaluated, and adapted. But these processes do not evolve in a pattern of clear-cut sequences; instead, the stages are constantly meshed and entangled in an ongoing process. Moreover, policies do not develop in a vacuum, but are adopted in a crowded policy space that leaves little space for policy innovation. Instead, new policies (only) modify, change, or supplement older policies, or—more likely— compete with them or contradict each other.

Hogwood and Peters (1983) suggested the notion of policy succession to highlight that new policies develop in a dense environment of already existing policies. Therefore, earlier policies form a central part of the systemic environment of policy-making; frequently other policies act as key obstacles for the adoption and implementation of a particular measure. At the same time, policies create side-effects and become the causes of later policy problems—across sectors (e.g., road construction leading to environmental problems) as well as within sectors (e.g., subsidies for agricultural products leading to overproduction)—and, hence, new policies themselves ("policy as its own cause,").

Despite its limitations, the policy cycle has developed into the most widely applied framework to organize and systemize the research on public policy. The policy cycle focuses attention on generic features of the policy process rather than on specific actors or institutions or particular substantial problems and respective programs. Thereby, the policy cycle highlighted the significance of the policy domain or subsystem as the key level of analysis. However, policy studies seldom apply the whole policy cycle framework as an analytical model that guides the selection of questions and variables. While a number of textbooks and some edited volumes are based on the cycle framework, academic debates in the field of policy studies have emerged from research related to particular stages of the policy process rather than on the whole cycle. Starting at different times in the development of the discipline, these different lines of research developed into more or less separate research communities following a distinct set of questions, analytical perspectives and methods. In other words, the policy cycle framework has guided policy analysis to generic themes of policy-making and has offered a device to structure empirical material; the framework has, however, not developed into a major theoretical or analytical program itself.

With these limitations of the policy cycle perspective in mind, the following briefly sketches theoretical perspectives developed to analyze particular stages of the cycle framework and highlights main research findings. While this overview does only offer a very limited and selective review of the literature, the account stresses how research related to particular stages has shaped the general understanding of the policy process and the policy cycle framework.

THE STAGES OF THE POLICY CYCLE

AGENDA-SETTING: PROBLEM RECOGNITION AND ISSUE SELECTION

Policy-making presupposes the recognition of a policy problem. Problem recognition itself requires that a social problem has been defined as such and that the necessity of state intervention has been expressed. The second step would be that the recognized problem is actually put on the agenda for serious consideration of public action (agenda-setting). The agenda is nothing more than "the list of subjects or problems to which governmental officials, and people outside the government closely associated with those officials, are paying some serious attention at any given time". The government's (or institutional) agenda has been distinguished from the wider media and the overall public (or systemic) agenda (**Cobb and Elder 1972**). While the government's (formal and informal) agenda presents the center of attention of studies on agenda-setting, the means and mechanisms of problem recognition and issue selection are tightly connected with the way a social problem is recognized and perceived on the public/media agenda.

As numerous studies since the 1960s have shown problem recognition and agenda-setting are inherently political processes in which political attention is attached to a subset of all possibly relevant policy problems. Actors within and outside government constantly seek to influence and collectively shape the agenda (e.g., by taking advantage of rising attention to a particular issue, dramatizing a problem, or advancing a particular problem definition). The involvement of particular actors (e.g., experts), the choice of institutional venues in which problems are debated and the strategic use of media coverage have been identified as tactical means to define issues. While a number of actors are involved in these activities of agenda control or shaping, most of the variables and mechanisms affecting agenda-setting lie outside the direct control of any single actor.

Agenda-setting results in a *selection* between diverse problems and issues. It is a process of structuring the policy issue regarding potential strategies and instruments that shape the development of a policy in the subsequent stages of a policy cycle. If the assumption is accepted that not all existing problems could receive the same level of attention the questions of the mechanisms of agenda-setting arise. What is perceived as a policy problem? How and when does a policy problem get on the government's agenda? And why are other problems excluded from the agenda? Moreover, issue attention cycles and tides of solutions connected to specific problems are relevant aspects of policy-studies concerned with agenda-setting.

Systematic research on agenda-setting first emerged as part of the critique of pluralism in the United States. One classic approach suggested that political debates and, hence, agenda-setting, emerge from confl ict between two actors, with the less politically powerful actor seeking to raise attention to the issue (conflict expansion). Others suggested that agenda-setting results from a process of filtering of issues and problems, resulting in non-decisions (issues and problems that are deliberately excluded from the formal agenda). Building on the seminal community power literature, policy-studies pointed out that non-decisions result from asymmetrical distribution of influence through institutional structures that exclude some issues from serious consideration of action.

The crucial step in this process of agenda-setting is the move of an issue from its recognition—frequently expressed by interested groups or affected actors—up to the formal political agenda.

This move encompasses several substages, in which succeeding selections of issues under conditions of scarce capacities of problem-recognition and problem-solving are made. Several studies of environmental policy development, for example, showed that it is not the objective problem load (e.g., the degree of air pollution) which explains the intensity of problem recognition and solving activities on the side of governments. Instead, a plausible definition of a problem and the creation of a particular policy image allowing to attach a particular solution to the problem, have been identified as key variables affecting agenda-setting.

While problem recognition and problem defi nition in liberal democracies are said to be largely conducted in public, in the media or at least among domain-specifi c professional (public) communities, the actual agenda-setting is characterized by different patterns in terms of actor composition and the role of the public. The *outside-initiation* pattern, where social actors force governments to place an issue on the systemic agenda by way of gaining public support, presents but one of different types of agenda-setting. Equally significant are processes of policies without public input such as when interest groups have direct access to government agencies and are capable of putting topics on the agenda without major interference or even recognition of the public (cf. May, 1991). The agriculture policy in certain European countries would be a classic example for such *inside-initiation* patterns of agenda-setting. Another pattern has been described as the *mobilization* of support within the public by the government after the initial agenda-setting has been accomplished without a relevant role for non-state actors (e.g., the introduction of the Euro or, rather, the campaign prior the implementation of the new currency).

Finally, **Howlett and Ramesh (2003, 141)** distinguish *consolidation* as a fourth type whereby state actors initiate an issue where public support is already high (e.g., German unifi cation). Despite the existence of different patterns of agenda-setting, modern societies are characterized by a distinctive role of the public/media for agenda-setting and policy-making, especially when novel types of problems (like risks) emerge (see **Hood, Rothstein, and Baldwin 2001**). Frequently, governments are confronted with forced choice situations (**Lodge and Hood, 2002**) where they simply cannot ignore public sentiment without risking the loss of legitimacy or credibility, and must give the issue some priority on the agenda. Examples range from incidents involving aggressive dogs, and Mad Cow Disease to the regulation of chemical substances (see **Lodge and Hood 2002; Hood, Rothstein, and Baldwin 2001**). While the mechanisms of agenda-setting do not determine the way the related policy is designed and implemented, policies following so-called knee-jerk responses of governments in forced choice situations tend to be combined with rather intrusive or coercive forms of state interventions. However, these policies frequently have a short life cycle or are recurrently object of major amendments in the later stages of the policy cycle after public attention has shifted towards other issues (**Lodge and Hood, 2002**).

The confluence of a number of interacting factors and variables determines whether a policy issue becomes a major topic on the policy agenda. These factors include both the material conditions of the policy environment (like the level of economic development), and the flow and cycle of ideas and ideologies, which are important in evaluating problems and connecting them with solutions (policy proposals). Within that context, the constellation of interest between the relevant actors, the capacity of the institutions in charge to act effectively, and the cycle of public problem perception as well as the solutions that are connected to the different problems are of central importance. While earlier models of agenda-setting have concentrated on the economic and social aspects as explanatory variables, more recent approaches stress the role of ideas, expressed in public and professional discourses (e.g., epistemic communities; **Haas 1992**), in shaping the perception of a particular problems. **Baumgartner and Jones (1993, 6)** introduced the notion of policy monopoly as the "monopoly on political understandings" of a particular policy problem and institutional arrangements reinforcing the particular "policy image"; they suggested that agenda-setting and policy change occurs when "policy monopolies" become increasingly contested and previously disinterested (or at least "non-active") actors are mobilized. Changing policy images are frequently linked to changing institutional "venues" within which issues are debated (**Baumgartner and Jones, 1993, 15; 2002, 19–23**).

How the different variables—actors, institutions, ideas, and material conditions—interact is highly contingent, depending on the specific situation. That also implies that agenda-setting is far from a rational selection of issues in terms of their relevance as a problem for the wider society. Instead, the shifting of attention and agendas (**Jones 2001, 145–47**) could eventually lead governments to adopt policies that contradict measures introduced earlier. The most influential model that tries to conceptualize the contingency of agenda-setting is Kingdon's multiple streams model that builds on the garbage can model of organizational choice. Kingdon introduced the notion of windows of opportunity that open up at a specific time for a specific policy. The policy window opens when three usually separate and independent streams—the policy stream (solutions), the politics stream (public sentiments, change in governments, and the like), and the problem stream (problem perception)—intersect. (The classical garbage can model distinguishes solutions, problems, actors, and decision opportunities.)

In a long-term perspective, attention cycles and the volatility of problem perception and reform moods for particular issues can be revealed. Within such cyclical processes, single issues appear on the agenda, will be removed later on, and may reappear on that agenda as part of a longer wave. Examples include the cyclical perception of environmental, consumer protection and criminal issues, in which (combined with economic and political conditions) single events (like accidents, disasters, and the like) could trigger agenda-setting.

A longitudinal perspective also points at changes in perceptions of a single issue, with some prior solutions later becoming problems (e.g., nuclear power). **Baumgartner and Jones (1993; 2002)** highlight the existence of both periods of stable policy agendas and periods of rapid change and take these findings as a starting point for the development of a policy process model (punctuated equilibrium) that challenges conventional notions of incrementalism.

POLICY FORMULATION AND DECISION-MAKING

During this stage of the policy cycle, expressed problems, proposals, and demands are transformed into government programs. Policy formulation and adoption includes the definition of objectives— what should be achieved with the policy—and the consideration of different action alternatives.

Some authors differentiate between formulation (of alternatives for action) and the final adoption (the formal decision to take on the policy). Because policies will not always be formalized into separate programs and a clear-cut separation between formulation and decision-making is very often impossible, we treat them as substages in a single stage of the policy cycle. In trying to account for different styles, patterns, and outcomes of policy formulation and decision-making, studies on this stage of the cycle framework have been particularly theory-oriented.

Over the last two decades or so, a fruitful connection with organizational decision theories has evolved (see Olsen 1991). A multiplicity of approaches and explanations has been utilized, ranging from pluralistic and corporatist interest intermediation to perspectives of incrementalism and the garbage can approach. Others are public choice approaches and the widely utilized neoinstitutionalist perspectives (both in its economical and historical-institutionalist variant; for an overview see **Parsons 1995, 134**).

At the same time, studies of policy formulation have long been strongly infl uenced by efforts to improve practices within governments by introducing techniques and tools of more rational decision- making. This became most evident during the heyday of political planning and reform policy in the 1960s and 1970s. Policy analysis was part of a reform coalition engaged in developing tools and methods for identifying effective and cost-effi cient policies (see Wittrock, Wagner, and **Wollmann 1991, 43–51**; **Wollmann 1984**). Western governments were strongly receptive to these ideas given the widespread confidence in the necessity and feasibility of long-term planning. Pioneered by attempts of the U.S. government to introduce Planning Programming Budgeting Systems (PPBS), European governments engaged in similar efforts of long-term planning.

Among parts of the policy research community and government actors, PPBS was perceived as a basis for rational planning and, hence, decision-making. The establishment of clearly defined goals, output targets within the budget statement, and the application of cost-benefit analysis to political programs were regarded as tools facilitating the definition of long-term political priorities.

From this perspective an ex-ante, rather rationalistic branch of policy analysis as analysis for policy developed, inspired by micro-economics and operational research (**Stokey and Zeckhauser 1978**).

Right from the beginning, these concepts of decision-making and political planning were heavily criticized from a political science background for being over-ambitious and technocratic ('rescuing policy analysis from PPBS', **Wildavsky 1969**). The role of economics and political science-based policy analysis in the wider reform debate of political planning provided a fertile ground for the prosperous development of the discipline. As policy advice (analysis for policy-making) became a major aspect of the planning euphoria during the 1970s, empirical research on decision-making practices (analysis of policy-making) was initiated for the first time (e.g., through the project group of governmental and administrative reform in Germany; **Mayntz and Scharpf 1975**).

Especially political scientists argued from the beginning (**Lindblom 1968; Wildavsky 1979**) that decision-making comprises not only information gathering and processing (analysis), but foremost consists of confl ict resolution within and between public and private actors and government departments (interaction). In terms of patterns of interdepartmental interaction, **Mayntz and Scharpf (1975)** argued that these usually follow the type of negative coordination (based on sequential participation of different departments after the initial policy program has been drafted) rather than ambitious and complex attempts of positive coordination (pooling suggested policy solutions as part of the drafting), thus leading to the typical process of reactive policy-making. The aim of political science based policy analysis was, therefore, to suggest institutional arrangements which would support more active policy-making.

While these (earlier) studies pointed to the crucial role of the ministerial bureaucracy and top civil servants in policy formulation (**Dogan 1975; Heclo and Wildavsky 1974**), governments and higher civil servants are not strictly separated from the wider society when formulating policies; instead, they are constantly interacting with social actors and form rather stable patterns of relationships (policy networks). Whereas the fi nal decision on a specifi c policy remains in the realm of the responsible institutions (mainly cabinet, ministers, Parliament), this decision is preceded by a more or less informal process of negotiated policy formation, with ministerial departments (and the units within the departments), organized interest groups and, depending on the political system, elected members of parliaments and their associates as major players. Numerous policy studies have convincingly argued that the processes in the preliminary stages of decision-making strongly influence the final outcome and very often shape the policy to a larger extend than the final processes within the parliamentary arena (Kenis and Schneider 1991). Moreover, these studies made a strong case against the rational model of decision-making. Instead of a rational selection among alternative policies, decision-making results from bargaining between diverse actors within a policy subsystem—the result being determined by the constellation and power resources of (substantial and institutional) interest of the involved actors and processes of partisan mutual adjustment. Incrementalism, thus, forms the typical style (Lindblom 1959, 1979) of this kind of policy formation, especially in allocation of budgets (Wildavsky 1964, 1988).

During the 70s and 80s, traditional theories of pluralism in policy-making (many, competing interests without privileged access) were, at least in Western Europe, substituted by theories of corporatist policy-making (few, privileged associations with strong infl uence, cf. Schmitter and **Lehmbruch, 1979**). At the same time, more elaborate theories of policy networks became prominent (**Heclo 1978; Marin and Mayntz, 1991**). Policy networks are, generally, characterized by nonhierarchical, horizontal relationships between actors inside the network. Generalized political exchange (**Marin 1990**) represents the characteristic mode of interaction and diffuse reciprocity (opposed to market-type direct reciprocity) is the corresponding social orientation of actors in the inner circle of networks. In contrast, a higher degree of conflict is to be expected as far as the access to these policy networks is concerned. However, as Sabatier (1991, cf. **Sabatier, Jenkins-Smith 1993, 1999**) stressed, a policy subsystem frequently consists of more than one network. The different networks (or advocacy coalitions) then compete for the dominance in the respective policy domain.

Despite the considerable level of self-governance within policy networks, governments still play a crucial role in influencing the actor constellation within these networks, for example by altering the portfolio of ministries, creating new ones or establishing/abolishing agencies. (The renaming of the German federal Ministry of Agriculture to the Ministry of Consumer Protection, Food, and Agriculture during the BSE [Bovine Spongiform Encephalopathy] crisis serves as an example of a deliberate attempt to break up long-established policy networks in the agriculture sector as a prerequisite for policy change. Similar changes occurred also in the UK.) One major reason for the strong inclination of ministerial bureaucracies to defend their turf lies in the linkage between the allocation of responsibilities within government and the venues provided for social actors to the policy-making system **(Wilson 1989).** While these access points are of crucial importance for social actors seeking to influence policy formulation, established relationships with interest groups at the same time provide the power-basis of departments in interdepartmental relationships and conflicts.

Any redistribution of organizational structures and institutional arrangements will favour some and discriminate against others and will, therefore, become a contested issue.

While patterns of interaction between governments and society in policy networks are regarded as an omnipresent phenomenon, the particular constellation of actors within policy networks vary between policy domains, as well as between nation states with different political/administrative cultures, traditions of law (cf. **Feick and Jann 1988**) and differences regarding the wider constitutional setting. As the historical-institutional approach in policy research has pointed out, countries have developed particular types of policy networks resulting from the interaction of the pre-existing state structure and the organization of society at critical junctures in history (**Lehmbruch 1991**). These differences are said to foster national styles of policy-making in terms of preferred policy instruments and patterns of interaction between state and society (**Richardson, Gustafsson, and Jordan 1982**; **Feick and Jann 1988**). It remains, however, a debated issue in comparative policy research if policy networks are to a larger degree shaped by the (different) basic national institutional patterns or if the policies within specific policy subsystems are, to a larger extent, shaped by sectoral, domain-specific governance structures (with the implication of more variety between sectors within one country than between countries regarding one sector) (see e.g., **Bovens, t'Hart, and Peters 2001**).

Some have argued that the emphasis on the pervasive nature of policy networks obscured national variations of patters of policy-making that are in fact related to (different) underlying institutional arrangements and state architectures (**Döhler and Manow 1995**).

In order to allow for the analysis of different structural patterns of state-society interaction, policy research has developed taxonomies of policy networks. While considerable variation (and maybe even confusion, cf. **Dowding 2001**) prevails, one major distinction has been made between iron triangles, sub-governments, or policy communities on the one hand and issue networks centered around a particular policy issues (e.g., abortion, fuel taxes, speed limits) on the other hand. These two basic types are differentiated along the dimensions of actor composition and the insulation of the network from the wider environment. Iron triangles typically consist of state bureaucracies, parliamentary (sub-) committees, and organized interests generally sharing policy objectives and ideas. Others suggested the notion of policy communities to emphasize the latter aspect of coherent world-views and shared policy objectives (however, the term has been defi ned in many ways, including a meaning that resembles the notion of issue networks). **Heclo (1978)** has contrasted iron triangles with issue networks consisting of a multitude of actors, and with comparatively open boundaries and a looser coupling between the actors involved.

When it comes to the final adoption of a particular policy option, the formal institutions of the governmental system move into the center. But even during this substage, modes of self-regulation, sometimes in the shadow of hierarchy, have increasingly been regarded as a widespread pattern of policy-making (**Mayntz and Scharpf 1995**). Which of the proposed policy options will be finally adopted depends on a number of factors; two of them should be highlighted. First, the feasible set of policy options is reduced by basic substantial parameters. Some policies are excluded because of scarcity of resources—not only in terms of economic resources, but also because political support presents a critical resource in the policy-making process. Second, the allocation of competencies between different actors (e.g., government) plays a crucial role in decision-making. For example, tax policy in Germany is one of the domains in which the federal government is not only dependent on the support of the Federal Parliament (Bundestag, which is most of the time assured in parliamentary systems), but also on the consent of the Federal Council (Bundesrat, the representation of the Länder governments). The scope for substantial policy changes is, all others things being equal, more restricted in federal systems, where second chambers of parliaments and also (more frequently) constitutional courts are in a position of the potential veto player (**Tsebelis 2002**). At the same time, subnational levels of government possess more leeway to initiate policies in countries with a federal or a decentralized structure than in centralized countries. Another crucial aspect of policy formulation represents the role of (scientific) policy advice.

While earlier models differentiated between technocratic (policy decisions depending on superior knowledge provided by experts) and decisionist (primacy of politics over science) models of the science/policy nexus (see **Wittrock 1991**), the dominant normative understanding favored a pragmatic and cooperative interaction at eye level (pragmatic model, see Habermas, 1968). Empirically, policy advice was recognized as a 'diffuse process of enlightenment', in which politicians and bureaucrats (contrary to conventional wisdom, especially in the academic world) are not infl uenced by single studies or reports. Instead, policy advice has an impact on the middle- and long-term changes of general problem perceptions and world views (**Weiss 1977**). Moreover, scientifi c research is only one of diverse sources of information and knowledge that is being brought into the policy-making process (**Lindblom and Cohen 1979, 10–29**).

Over the last years, the role of think tanks in these processes has formed a focal point in debates on changing ways of policy-making, for example in the formulation of neoliberal policies in the 1980s (**Weiss 1992**). Think tanks and international organizations are regarded as catalysts fostering the exchange and transfer of policy ideas, solutions, and problem perceptions between governments and beyond (**Stone 2004**). Some have argued that policy transfer has become a regular, though distinctive, part of contemporary policy formulation (**Dolowitz and Marsh 2000**). However, while the practice and existence of processes of transfer and learning are hardly deniable, the literature has difficulties in drawing clear boundaries between policy transfer and other aspects of policy-making, especially as the notion of lesson drawing (as one pattern of policy transfer) resembles the rational model of decision-making (cf. **James and Lodge 2003**). The study of policy transfer and learning has been advanced by insights drawn from organizational theory, in particular the notion of institutional isomorphism that differentiates between coercive, mimetic and professional mechanisms of emulation (**DiMaggio and Powell 1991**; for applications see, among others, **Lodge and Wegrich, 2005b; Jann 2004; Lodge 2003**).

Most studies dealing with the role of knowledge in policy formulation agree that, in the contemporary age, knowledge is more widely spread beyond the boundaries of (central) governments than some decades ago. Experts and international institutions (like the Organization for Economic Co-operation and Development [OECD]) are said to play an increasingly visible role in communicating knowledge within the public debate on political issues (**Albaek, Christiansen, and Togeby 2003**). Therefore, the perception of a monopoly of information on the side of the bureaucracy (**Max Weber's *Dienst- and Herrschaftswissen***) is obsolete. Policy formulation, at least in western democracies, proceeds as a complex social process, in which state actors play an important but not necessarily decisive role.

IMPLEMENTATION

The decision on a specific course of action and the adoption of a program does not guarantee that the action on the ground will strictly follow policy makers' aims and objectives. The stage of execution or enforcement of a policy by the responsible institutions and organizations that are often, but not always, part of the public sector, is referred to as implementation. Policy implementation is broadly defined as "what happens between the establishment of an apparent intention on the part of the government to do something, or to stop doing something, and the ultimate impact in the world of action" (**O'Toole 2000, 266**). This stage is critical as political and administrative action at the frontline are hardly ever perfectly controllable by objectives, programs, laws, and the like (**cf. Hogwood and Gunn 1984**). Therefore, policies and their intentions will very often be changed or even distorted; its execution delayed or even blocked altogether.

An ideal process of policy implementation would include the following core elements:

- Specification of program details (i.e., how and by which agencies/organizations should the program be executed? How should the law/program be interpreted?);
- Allocation of resources (i.e., how are budgets distributed? Which personnel will execute the program? Which units of an organization will be in charge for the execution?);
- Decisions (i.e., how will decisions of single cases be carried out?).

The detection of the implementation stage as a missing link (**Hargrove 1975**) in the study of policymaking can be regarded as one of the most important conceptual innovations of policy research in the 1970s. Earlier, implementation of policies was not recognized as a separate stage within or element of the policy-making process. What happens after a bill becomes a law (**Bardach 1977**) was not perceived as a central problem—not for the decision makers and, therefore, also not for policy analysis. The underlying assumption was that governments pass laws, and this is where the core business of policy-making ends.

This perception has fundamentally changed since the seminal study by **Pressman and Wildavsky (1984 [1973])** on the implementation of a program targeting unemployment among members of minority groups in Oakland, California. Subsequently, the study of implementation as a core and often critical stage of the policy-making process became widespread currency. The starting point of Pressman and Wildavsky's analysis of the substeps involved in the implementation of the federal program, that was part of the ambitious social policy reform agenda put forth by President Johnson, was the unexpected failure of the program. Based on the analysis of the multitude of decision and clearing points at which involved actors were able to infl uence the policy along the lines of their particular interests, any successful policy implementation seemed to be more surprising than implementation failure (note the subtitle, *How Great Expectations in Washington Are Dashed in Oakland, or Why It's Amazing that Federal Programs Work at All*).

Following the path-breaking study, implementation research developed into *the* central field of policy research in the 1970s and early 1980s. Initially, implementation was regarded from a perspective that was later called the top-down approach. Implementation studies followed the hierarchical and chronological path of a particular policy and sought to assess how far the centrally defined goals and objectives are achieved when it comes to implementation. Most studies centered on those factors leading to deviations from these objectives. Intra- and inter-organizational coordination problems and the interaction of field agencies with the target group ranked as the most prominent variables accounting for implementation failures. Another explanation focused the policy itself, acknowledging that unsuccessful policy implementation could not only be the result of bad implementation, but also bad policy design, based on wrong assumptions about cause-effect relationships (cf. **Pressman and Wildavsky 1984 [1973]; Hogwood and Gunn 1984).**

Implementation studies of the fi rst generation thus shared a hierarchical, top-down understanding of governance, at least as a normative yardstick for the assessment of outcomes of implementation.

Implementation research was interested in developing theories about what works. One way to do this has been to assess the effectiveness of different types of policy instruments based on particular theories about cause and effect relations. Policy instruments have been classifi ed into regulatory, financial, informational, and organizational policy tools **(cf. Hood 1983; Mayntz 1979; Vedung 1998, see Salomon, 2002,** for a more differentiated classifi cation). One of the most prominent outcomes of the policy instruments perspective in implementation research has been the importance of the relationship between tool selection and policy implementation: Different policy instruments are vulnerable to specific types of implementation problems, with regulatory policies being aligned with control problems and subsidies with windfall gains on the side of the target group (see **Mayntz 1979).** Another result of this line of research has been that the reliance on wrong theories about cause and effect relations frequently leads to negative side-effects or even reverse effects of state interventions (see **Sieber 1981**).

Since the mid 1970s, implementation studies based on the top-down perspective have been increasingly challenged on analytical grounds, as well as in terms of their normative implications (see **Hill and Hupe 2002,** 51–57). Empirical evidence, showing that implementation was not appropriately described as a hierarchical chain of action leading directly from a decision at the center to the implementation in some fi eld agency, provided the ground for a competing concept of implementation.

The so-called bottom-up perspective suggested a number of analytical reorientations that subsequently became accepted in the wider implementation and policy literature. First, the central role of implementation agencies and their personnel in shaping the actual policy outcome has been acknowledged (street level bureaucracy, **Lipsky 1980**); in particular the pattern of coping with diverse and often contradictory demands associated with policies is a recurring theme in this line of research (see also **Lin 2000; Hill 2003; deLeon and deLeon 2002**). Second, the focus on single policies regarded as inputs into the implementation process was supplemented, if not replaced, by a perspective that regarded policy as the outcome of implementation resulting from the interaction of different actors *and* different programs. Elmore (1979/80) suggested the notion of backward mapping for a corresponding research strategy that begins at the last possible stage, when "administrative actions intersects with private choices" (**Elmore 1979/80, 604**). Third, the increasingly widespread recognition of linkages and networks between a number of (governmental and social) actors within a particular policy domain, cutting across the implementation/policy formulation borderline, provided the ground for the eventual abandonment of the hierarchical understanding of state/society interaction.

In sum, implementation research played a major role in triggering the move of policy research away from a state-centered endeavor, which was primarily interested in enhancing the internal administrative and governmental capacities and in fi ne-tuning program design and implementation.

Since the late 1980s, policy research is primarily interested in patterns of state-society interaction and has shifted its attention toward the institutional set-up of organizational fi elds in the wider society (e.g., the health, education, or science section). Based on the multiplicity of empirical studies in numerous policy areas, the classic leitmotiv of hierarchical governance has been abandoned. Policy networks and negotiated modes of coordination between public and private actors are not only (analytically) regarded as a pervasive pattern underlying contemporary policy-making, but also (normatively) perceived as an effective mode of governance that refl ects conditions of modern societies. Studies of policy-making were decreasingly following the traditional stages model, but encompassed all kinds of actors in the organizational and regulatory field, thereby undermining the policy cycle framework.

EVALUATION AND TERMINATION

Policy-making is supposed to contribute to problem solving or at least to the reduction of the problem load. During the evaluation stage of the policy cycle, these intended outcomes of policies move into the center of attention. The plausible normative rationale that, finally, policy-making should be appraised against intended objectives and impacts forms the starting point of policy evaluation.

But, evaluation is not only associated with the final stage in the policy cycle that either ends with the termination of the policy or its redesign based on modified problem perception and agenda-setting.

At the same time, evaluation research forms a separate subdiscipline in the policy sciences that focuses on the intended results and unintended consequences of policies. Evaluation studies are not restricted to a particular stage in the policy cycle; instead, the perspective is applied to the whole policy-making process and from different perspectives in terms of timing (ex ante, ex post).

Evaluation research emerged in the United States in the context of political controversies centered on the social reform programs of the Great Society of the 1960s. This early debate was concerned with methodological issues and sought to demonstrate its own relevance (**cf. Weiss 1972; Levine et al. 1981; Wholey 1983**). Evaluation research subsequently spread across OECD countries and was concerned with the activities of the interventionist welfare state **(Albaek 1998)** and reform policies in general. Evaluation was, for example, perceived as a way to systematically apply the idea of experimental testing of (new) policy options in a controlled setting **(Hellstern and Wollmann 1983).** Despite the inclination of evaluation research toward a rigorous application of quantitative research tools and quasi-experimental research designs, the general problem of isolating the infl uence and impact of a specifi c policy measure on policy outcomes has not been solved (given the variety of variables shaping policy outcomes). Moreover, attempts to establish evaluation exercises as part of politics-free policy-making have been widely regarded as failures. Their results were contested as being largely dependent on the inherent and often implicit values on which the evaluation was based (see, e.g., **Fischer 1990**).

Moreover, the role of evaluation in the policy process goes far beyond the scope of scientific evaluation studies. Policy evaluation takes place as a regular and embedded part of the political process and debate. Therefore, scientific evaluation has been distinguished from administrative evaluations conducted or initiated by the public administration and political evaluation carried out by diverse actors in the political arena, including the wider public and the media **(cf. Howlett and Ramesh 2003, 210–16).** Not only scientific studies, but also government reports, the public debate and activities of respective opposition parties embrace substantial elements of evaluation. Also the classical forms of overseeing government and public services in liberal democracies by law courts and legislators as well as audit offices can be grouped as evaluations.

While evaluation research sought to establish evaluation as a central part of rational evidence-based policy-making, activities of evaluation are particularly exposed to the specific logic and incentives of political processes in at least two major ways, both of them related to blame games

(**Hood 2002**). First, the assessment of policy outputs and outcomes is biased according to the position and substantial interest, as well as the values, of a particular actor. In particular, the shifting of blame for poor performance is a regular part of politics. Second, fl awed definition of policy aims and objectives presents a major obstacle for evaluations. Given the strong incentive of blame-avoidance, governments are encouraged to avoid the precise defi nition of goals because otherwise politicians would risk taking the blame for obvious failure. Even outside constellations that may be seen as shaped by partisan politics, the possibility of a self-evaluating organization has been strongly contested, because it confl icts with some of the fundamental values and interests of organizations (e.g., stability; **Wildavsky 1972**).

Evaluations can lead to diverse patterns of policy-learning, with different implications in terms of feed-back mechanisms and a potential restart of the policy process. One pattern would be that successful policies will be reinforced; a pattern that forms the core idea of so-called pilot projects (or model experiment), in which a particular measure is fi rst introduced within a (territorial, substantive, or temporal) limited context and only extended if the evaluation is supporting. Prominent examples range from school reforms, the introduction of speed limits (and related measures in the field of transport policy), to the whole fi eld of genetic engineering. However, instead of enhancing evidence-based policy-making, pilot projects may represent tools that are utilized for purposes of conflict avoidance; contested measures are not finally adopted but taken up as a pilot projects and thereby postponed until the political mood is ripe for a more enduring course of action.

Evaluations could also lead to the termination of a policy. Reform concepts and management instruments like Sunset Legislation and Zero-Based-Budgeting (ZBB) have been suggested as key tools that encourage terminating prior policies in order to allow for new political priorities to materialize. ZBB is supposed to replace traditional incremental budgeting (the annual continuation of budget items with minor cuts and increases reflecting political moods and distribution of power).

Instead, a new budget should be developed for single policy areas (and the responsible agencies) that expires at a predetermined date (sunset). All programs have to be periodically reassessed, designed, and budgeted. While ZBB proved to be overtly rationalistic and technocratic and, therefore, remained a short-lived reform idea, the notion of sunset legislation has regained more widespread currency (at least on the level of reform debates) since the mid-1990s in connection with the so called regulatory policy agenda (OECD 2002).

The primary idea of policy termination—a policy problem has been solved or the adopted policy measures have been recognized to be ineffective in dealing with the set policy goals— seems rather difficult to enforce under real-world conditions of policy-making (see **Bardach**

1976; Behn 1978; deLeon 1978; Kaufman 1976). Rather large-scale budget cuts (e.g., related to subsidies) or windows of opportunity (e.g., changing governments, public sentiments) could trigger policy termination (**Geva-May 2004**). These processes are frequently connected with partisan motivations, like the implementation of election promises (see the change in energy policy introduced at the beginning of President George W. Bush's fi rst term, or the first Schröder government's withdrawal of pension reforms introduced by the Kohl-Government in Germany).

However, the literature on policy termination suggests that attempts of policy termination are neither widespread nor successful in overcoming resistance of infl uential actors, allowing for the growth of a "Jurassic Park of programs" (**Pollitt 2003, 113**). Studies of policy termination, therefore, are frequently concerned with why policies and programs "live on" although they have "outlived their usefulness" (**Geva-May 2004, 309**). Counter-strategies against termination efforts range from window-dressing activities (instead of substantial changes) to the formation of crosscutting anti-termination coalitions formed by benefi ciaries of programs (e.g., delivery agencies, affected interest groups, local politicians; **Bardach 1976**). These coalitions can rely on a comparative advantage, because they are easier able to overcome collective action problems than any protermination coalition (given the threat of a potential loss of resources provided by the policy). In addition, politicians face greater incentives towards the declaration of new programs rather than the termination of old ones that include the admission of failures. The short-term political, as well as fi nancial, costs of termination may outweigh the long-term benefi ts (**cf. Bardach 1979; deLeon 1978; Geva-May 2004**).

Apart from cases of unsuccessful termination, dynamic developments of policy booms (**Dunleavy, 1986**) as well as phenomena of extinction and reversal (**Hood 1994**) are alternative patterns of policy development. Among the most important variables accounting for policy reversals (the most important ones being economic policy changes since the late 1970s) are changing ideas and political coalitions supporting a new packaging of policy problems and solutions.

Overall, the analysis of the final stage of the policy cycle has witnessed a substantial departure from its initial focus on evaluation towards wider issues of policy change and inertia and the variables affecting these patterns.

Critique

While the numerous empirical studies and theoretical debates concerned with *single* stages of the policy cycle have substantially contributed to a better understanding of the prerequisites, elements, and consequences of policy-making, they also have triggered a rising critique challenging the underlying policy cycle framework. This critique is primarily questioning the analytical differentiation of the policy process into separate and discrete stages and sequences. As mentioned above, implementation research has played a crucial role in preparing the ground for that critique; implementation studies revealed that a clear-cut separation between policy formation and implementation is hardly reflecting real-world policy-making, neither in terms of any hierarchical or chronological sequence (first formation, then implementation), nor in terms of the involved actors.

Starting from empirical observations referring to single aspects of the cycle model an increasingly fundamentalist critique evolved, challenging the whole cycle framework. The approach was named, rather polemically, the textbook approach (**Nakamura 1987**). While the role of the stages heuristic in transforming political research and allowing the analysis of different stages of the policy process involving various institutional actors has been acknowledged even by its fiercest critics, it is said that the model has outlived its usefulness and should be replaced by more advanced models (**Sabatier 1999**). According to Sabatier, the uncritical application of the stages model prevents scientific progress rather than promotes it. Calls for the utilization of alternative frameworks and theories have criticized the stage heuristic in particular on these grounds (**cf. Sabatier 1999; Sabatier, Jenkins-Smith, 1993**):

- With regard to description, the stages model is said to suffer from descriptive inaccuracy because empirical reality does not fi t with the classifi cation of the policy process into discrete and sequential stages. Implementation, for example, affects agenda-setting; or a policy will be reformulated while some field agencies try to enforce ambiguous programs; or policy termination has to be implemented. In a number of cases it is more or less impossible, or at least not useful, to differentiate between stages. In other cases, the sequence is reversed; some stages miss completely or fall together.

- In terms of its conceptual value, the policy cycle lacks defi ning elements of a theoretical framework. In particular, the stages model does not offer causal explanations for the transition between different stages. Hence, studies of particular stages draw on a number of different theoretical concepts that have not been derived from the cycle framework itself. The specific models developed to explain processes within single stages were not connected to other approaches referring to other stages of the policy cycle.

The policy cycle is based on an implicit top-down perspective, and as such, policy-making will be framed as a hierarchical steering by superior institutions. And the focus will always be on single programs and decisions and on the formal adoption and implementation of these programs. The interaction between diverse programs, laws, and norms and their parallel implementation and evaluation does not gain the primary attention of policy analysis.

Moreover, by adopting the policy cycle perspective, the elements of the policy process that are not related to problem-solving activities are systematically ignored. Symbolic or ritual activities and activities purely related to the maintenance of power (**Edelman 1971**) do not feature in the stages model. However, rather than being the main objective of political action, policy-making frequently results as a by-product of politics. While the political process could be analyzed in terms of its impact on problem-solving, this should not be confused with an interpretation that regards actors as primarily taking a problem-solving orientation. Finally, the policy cycle framework ignores the role of knowledge, ideas and learning in the policy process as infl uential independent variables affecting all stages of the policy process (and not only in the evaluation stage). Overall, the cycle framework leads toward an oversimplified and unrealistic world-view.

Policy-making appears to be too straightforward; the whole process is reduced to initiating and continuing programs. As mentioned earlier, the role of prior policies in shaping policy-making as well as the interaction between diverse cycles, stages and actors is not systematically taken into account. However, a central feature of the policy process in modern societies is the interaction between policy-related activities at different levels (local, regional, national, inter- and supranational) and arenas (governmental, parliamentary, administrative, scientifi c communities, and the like) of governance. Policies are constantly debated, implemented, enforced, and evaluated. For example, environmental policy-making in the United States and in the European Union is not appropriately understood without the acknowledgement of interaction between initiatives from the different levels of government and without taking the impact of activities in other policy areas (e.g., transport, energy, or the wider economic policy) into account. Even the assumption of clearly defined and separated policy subsystems seems to be unrealistic.

The fundamental critique of Sabatier and others has triggered the development of alternative approaches beside. The advocacy coalition framework developed by Sabatier, the multiple-stream framework, the institutional rational choice approach, policy diffusion models, and the punctuated equilibrium theory are regarded as particularly promising alternative frameworks (see **Sabatier1999**).

LIMITATIONS AND UTILITY OF THE POLICY CYCLE PERSPECTIVE

With that fundamental critique in mind, what would be an overall assessment of the limitations and the utility of the policy cycle framework? First of all, most of the different single points of criticism are reasonable. Like any framework, the cycle framework draws an extremely simplified picture of reality, highlighting some aspects while disregarding others. Above all, the policy cycle does not offer a causal model of the policy process with clearly defi ned dependent and independent variables. Therefore, the policy cycle or stages perspective could, according to Sabatier, not act as a theoretical framework of the policy process.

However, as **Renate Mayntz** has already emphasized in 1983, policy research is not only, and frequently not primarily concerned with the application of the analytical scientifi c theory (*analytische Wissenschafts-therorie*) (testing hypothesis, causal relations between variables) (see the debate on different logics of research in Brady and Collier 2004). Instead, the detailed and differentiated understanding of the internal dynamic and peculiarities of complex processes of policy-making counts as distinctive and relevant objectives of policy research (**Mayntz 1983, 14)**.

Against these objectives, the policy cycle perspective has proven to provide an excellent heuristic device. Studies following the policy cycle perspective have enhanced our understanding of the complex preconditions, central factors infl uencing, and diverse outcomes of the policy process.

The diverse concepts developed in studies seeking to understand specifi c parts of the policy cycle have offered a number of useful tools to classify various elements of the whole process. Hence, the policy cycle perspective will continue to provide an important conceptual framework in policy research, as long as the heuristic purpose of the framework is considered and the departure from the hierarchical top-down perspective and the receptivity for other and new approaches in the wider political science literature is taken into account. The cycle framework also fulfills a vital role in structuring the vast amount of literature, the abundance of theoretical concepts, analytical tools and empirical studies, and therefore is not only crucial for teaching purposes (**Parsons 1995, 80**). The framework is also essential as a basic (background) template for assessing and comparing the particular contributions (and omissions) of more recent theories of the policy process. Therefore, the critique of the policy cycle, which is centered on general criteria for frameworks, theories and models, neglects the crucial role of the perspective in providing a base-line for the 'communication' between the diverse approaches in the fi eld. In that respect, we agree with **Schlager (1999, 239, 258)**, who highlights the openness of the cycle perspective for different theoretical and empirical interests in the field of policy studies (and agree with the critique of any application of the cycle perspective as a theoretical framework or model in a strict sense), but would add and emphasize the vital role of the cycle perspective for the integration of the diverse literature.

Numerous empirical studies and theoretical considerations have been conducted along the lines of single stages; these studies made important contributions not only to the policy literature, but also to the wider political science literature. For example, the whole debate on (new forms of) governance and the development from government to governance builds on results of and debates within policy research (**Jann 2003; Lodge and Wegrich 2005a, b**). Research on implementation has prepared the ground for the governance debate by detecting non-hierarchical modes of governance and patterns of co-governance between state and social actors, and through the recognition of the crucial role of civil society (organizations) for policy delivery.

Central research questions in the academic policy literature as well as in applied research are (more or less explicitly) still derived from the heuristic offered by the policy cycle framework. Questions concerning the actual impacts of particular interventions (evaluation) or concerned with the consequences following from the results of evaluations (termination, new problem perception and recognition) will remain important ones. The same applies to the other stages of the policy process; of course, it is still of central importance if and why a policy drifts away from the original design during implementation, or which actors are the most important ones in defi ning a policy problem or during the formal adoption of a particular policy.

In terms of democratic governance and from the perspective of public administration research, it remains of central relevance in which stage which actors are dominant and which are not. Which role do parties, parliaments, the media, interest groups, single agencies, or scientific communities play in defining which problems should be addressed or how laws should be applied and enforced?

Could it be that, contrary to our normative models, crucial policies are formulated without major interference of elected politicians, which then are only capable to initiate minor adaptations during implementation? The risk exists that empirical fi ndings concerning the complex policy process—pictured as a densely entangled space in which numerous parallel processes operate with frequent interactive feedback loops—leads to the negligence of these central research questions concerning actors' different roles in the different stages of the policy process. Elected officials and appointed bureaucrats, interest groups and corporations, and scientists and experts have different responsibilities in democratic processes—and these roles are linked to the different stages of the policy process, with the maturity of the respective policy.

Therefore, the policy cycle framework does not only offer a yardstick for the evaluation of the (comparative) success or failure of a policy; it also offers a perspective against which the democratic quality of these processes could be assessed (without following the assumption of a simple, discrete sequence and clear separation of stages). Additionally, the cycle framework allows the use of different analytical perspectives and corresponding research questions that will stay among the most important ones in policy research, although the stages heuristic of the policy cycle does not offer a comprehensive causal explanation for the whole policy process and even if the fundamental theoretical assumptions, on which initial versions of the framework were based, have long been left behind; of course, it is still of central importance if and why a policy drifts away from the original design during implementation. Similarly, it is still a relevant question, which actors are the most important in defining a policy problem or formally adopting a particular policy.

4.5. THEORETICAL APPROACHES TO STUDY THE POLICY MAKING PROCESS AND THE POLITICAL FOUNDATIONS OF MAIN ACTORS

Participants vary in how they view the policy process and in what they seek to gain from it. At a minimum we can identify rationalists, technicians, incrementalists, and reformists. All four types of actors will typically be involved in any complex issue. However, at any one time or for any one issue, one or more of the groups may dominate. The four types of participants vary in the roles they play in the policy process, the values they seek to promote, the source of goals for each, and their operating styles. [26]

4.5.1. RATIONALISTS

"The main characteristic of rationalists is that they involve reasoned choices about the desirability of adopting different courses of action to resolve public problems."[27] This process of reasoned choice 1) identifies the problem, 2) defines and ranks goals, 3) identifies all policy alternatives, 4) forecasts consequences of each alternative, 5) compares consequences in relationship with goals, and 6) chooses the best alternative.[28] This approach is associated with the role of the planner and professional policy analyst, whose training stresses rational methods in treating public problems.

Often the methods themselves are valued by the rationalist and therefore are promoted. It is assumed that goals are discoverable in advance and that "perfect information" is available.[29] The operating style tends to be that of the comprehensive planner; that is, one who seeks to analyze all aspects of the issue and test all possible alternatives by their effects and contribution to the stated goals. Most readers probably find this approach appealing. It strikes one as commonsensical to be as comprehensive as possible. Unfortunately, both institutional and political characteristics frequently interfere with the realization of so-called rational goals.

4.5.2. TECHNICIANS

A technician is really a type of rationalist, one engaged in the specialized work associated with the several stages of decision making. Technicians may well have discretion, but only within a limited sphere. They normally work on projects that require their expertise but are defined by others. The role they play is that of the specialist of expert called in for a particular assignment. The values they promote are those associated with their professional training, for example, as engineers, physicists, immunologists, or statisticians. Goals are typically set by others, perhaps any of the other three types identified here (or a mix of them). the operating style of the technician tends to be abstracted from that on the rationalist (who tends to be comprehensive). The technician displays confidence within the limits of training and experience but considerable discomfort if called upon to make more extensive judgments. [30]

4.5.3. INCREMENTALISTS

Charles Jones associates incrementalism with politicians in our policy system. Politicians tend to be critical of or impatient with planners and technicians, though, dependent on what they produce. Incrementalists doubt that comprehensiveness and rationality are possible in this most imperfect world. They see policy development and implementation as a "serial process of constant adjustment to the outcomes (proximate and long-range) of action."[31]

For incrementalists, information and knowledge are never sufficient to produce a complete policy program. They tend to be satisfied with increments, with building on the base, with working at the margins. The values associated with this approach are those of the past or of the status quo. Policy for incrementalists tends to be a gradual unfolding. Goals emerge as a consequence of demands, either for doing something new or, more typically, for making adjustments in what is already on the books. Finally, the operating style of incrementalists is that of the bargainer-constantly hearing demands, testing intensities, and proposing compromises.[32]

4.5.4. REFORMISTS

Reformists are like incrementalists in accepting the limits of available information and knowledge in the policy process, but are quite different in the conclusions they draw. Incrementalists judge that these limits dictate great caution in making policy moves. As David Braybrooke and Charles Lindblom note, "Only those policies are considered whose known or expected consequences differ incrementally from the status quo."[33]

This approach is much too conservative for reformists who, by nature, want to see social change. They would agree with David Easton that "we need to accept the validity of addressing ourselves directly to the problems of the day to obtain quick, short-run answers with the tools and generalizations currently available, however inadequate they may be."[34] The emphasis is on acting now because of the urgency of problems. This is the approach taken by self-styled citizen lobbyists. The values are those related to social change, sometimes for its own sake but more often associated with the special interests of particular groups. Goals are set within the group by various processes, including the personal belief that the present outcomes of government action are just plain wrong. The operating style of reformists has become very activist, often involving demonstrations and confrontation.

Given the striking differences among these four types of participants it is not surprising that each group in highly critical of the others. It is alleged, for example, that rationalists simply do not understand human nature. Braybrooke and Lindblom state that the rationalist's "ideal is not adapted to man's limited problem-solving capacities."[35] Technicians are criticized for their narrowness. Incrementalists rely too much on the status quo and fail to evaluate their own decisions. Reformists are indicted for their unrealistic demands and uncompromising nature.Different eras do appear to evoke different perspectives: the incrementalism of the 1950s, the reformism of the 1960s and 1970s, the rationalism of the late 1970s and the early 1980s (particularly in energy, environmental, and economic planning). But in every era our politics is characterized by a mix of participants within and among the institutions. Thus each group is forced at some point to deal with or encounter the others. The product may favor one perspective at a given stage of the policy process, but the multiplicity of institutions, governments, and decision making insures a melding over time.

Table 3: Four Perspectives in Public Policy Analysis

Perspective	CharacteristicsRoles	Values	Goals	Style	Criticism
Rationalist	Policy Analyst/Planner	Method	Discover	Comprehensive	Failure to acknowledge limits
Technician	Expert / Specialist	Training / Expertise	Set by others	Explicit	Narrowness
Incrementalist	Politician	Status quo	Set by new demands	Bargaining	Conservative

Source: Jones, Ch. Ob.Cit. p. 32.

4.6 PUBLIC POLICY MAKING IN INDIA: ISSUES AND REMEDIES

Public policy-making in India has frequently been characterized by a failure to anticipate needs, impacts, or reactions which could have reasonably been foreseen, thus impeding economic development. Policies have been reversed or changed more frequently than warranted by exogenous changes or new information. This section is concerned with why India's policymaking structures have so much difficulty in formulating the "right" policy and then sticking to it. It goes on to ask, and make a modest beginning in answering, the question of what can be done to improve the structures and systems involved in the making of public policy in India.

The making of public policy for a country as large, populous and diverse as India is intrinsically a more complex task than in a smaller political unit. This makes a study of the institutions which make policy all the more important. Measured by economic growth or attainment of human development objectives, India remains not only an underdeveloped country but one which is usually regarded as an under-performer, which could do better.

If it is taken as given that India is an under-performer, the question then arises as to why is this the case. *A priori*, under-performance vis-a-vis potential could be due to

- adopting the wrong public policies
- poorly implementing the right public policies.

There can, of course, be valid disagreements as to what is the "right" policy in a given sector, in a given situation. It can be argued that merely because there are errors, changes or postponements in policies, one cannot conclude that policy-making suffers from weakness. Success is often the result of trial and error. Disagreements, often strong ones, are common and, in a democratic society, both inevitable and healthy. Vigorous debate prior to policy-making and adaptation in response to debate is good, not bad. Flexibility in policymaking to respond to evolving exogenous factors is good, not bad. And the phenomenon of political considerations intervening in decisions otherwise well taken, is inevitable in a fractious but genuinely democratic polity like India. A survey of some recent and not-so-recent examples of policy-making in India suggests however, that there may indeed be something wrong with the policymaking process:-

I. POLICY ON PRIVATE POWER

In 1991, in the wake of the then newly-launched liberalisation process, the Central Government decided to permit private participation in the power sector by "Independent Power Producers". The 1991 policy allowed states to enter into Memoranda of Understanding with individual promoters without following open or competitive tendering. A number of states entered into these MOUs, and the Central Government also committed itself to providing 'counter-guarantees' to the project promoters of these so-called "fast track" projects. The nowdefunct Enron plant in Dabhol was the biggest of these projects. As is now known, the Dabhol project was a disaster, and indeed the 1991 approach is now almost universally acknowledged to have been severely faulty. There has been a lot of criticism of the detailed terms of the agreements on the Dabhol project and other individual MOU/fast track projects. However, the most important cause of the independent power fiasco was the poorly crafted policy, which (among other things) failed to take account of the problems in the distribution and supply side of the industry, the scope for mispricing in a non-competitive process and the lessons learnt in other countries in private power development.

II. Grounding of Airbus Aircraft

In 1990, a newly purchased Airbus A 320 aircraft of Indian Airlines crashed killing many passengers. The Central Government decided to ground all the newly acquired aircraft on suspicion that a design defect in the aircraft might be the cause of the crash. In the initial aftermath of the crash, the decision could be considered an understandable short-term precaution, but the decision was allowed to stand for several months. The grounding forced Indian Airlines to lease aircraft from charter operators and caused crippling losses from which it did not fully recover for many years. Eventually the planes were allowed to fly without any modification. With hindsight, the long stoppage was a serious policy error, which could have been avoided by a better policymaking process.

III. Value Added Tax (VAT)

There have been repeated postponements of the introduction of VAT despite years of preparation1. Till late March 2003, it was assumed that VAT would be2 introduced on April 1st 2003. This was then postponed to June 1st3. Eventually this too was deferred, for a variety of reasons4, and the target date has been extended to April 1st 2005 . Last minute changes have been made to policy decisions (for example on retaining exemptions for new industries) which were taken after long deliberation. Uncertainties about scope remained and reached a stage where a strike by truckers listed exemption from VAT as a demand8, when in fact they were never within its scope—a fact which was clarified later.

IV. Fiscal Responsibility Bill

A Fiscal Responsibility and Budget Management Bill was tabled in Parliament in 2000 to be enacted that year. It was eventually enacted only in 2003 in a greatly modified form.

V. Reservation of Parliamentary Seats for Women

Two attempts to introduce the Women's Reservation Bill over a three year period have failed. Both the main national political parties claim to be in support of the objective. Surprisingly alternatives to some of the specific policy provisions of the Bill, or the fundamental philosophical questions of the desirability or otherwise of reservation for women, do not seem to have been adequately explored or debated either before or after the first attempt at its introduction, or in the interregnum before the first and second attempt.

VI. TELECOM INTERCONNECTION CHARGES

The Telecom Regulatory Authority of India introduced a new policy on interconnection charges for private operators in April 2003. Within ten days of its introduction, after criticism from some of the affected quarters, it indicated that the policy would be changed.

VII. CONDITIONAL ACCESS SYSTEM (CAS)

The government decided in early 2003 to introduce a Conditional Access System for cable television in the metro cities with effect from July 15th 2003. The date was announced well in advance and due publicity given. All parties concerned were told that the policy was firm and as late as June 30, it was asserted that the date would not be changed. Various sections of the cable industry argued for or against various aspects of the policy. Among other things a shortage of set-top boxes was feared. Eventually, just a few days before July 15th, the implementation was postponed to September and it was decided to go for a phased implementation. After the postponement of the implementation to September, a Parliamentary Committee recommended even further postponement (this was not accepted by the Government). In September 2003, it was implemented in Chennai alone, but not in Delhi, Kolkata or Mumbai. As of mid-2004, the system continues to operate in Chennai alone (despite Chennai residents' judicial attempts to reverse it) but nowhere else.

In each of the above examples,

- Debate has occurred *after* policy-making, instead of before
- Views of one or other important party affected by a decision seem to have not been adequately considered or canvassed before policy was made
- considered decisions on relatively apolitical issues have been reversed at the last minute even where no new information or circumstances have arisen
- Factors which were endogenous to the problem, which were known or could have been foreseen while making policy, appear to have not been anticipated or considered.

These features are symptomatic of a poor policy-making process and in particular of "executive policy unreliability" [Evans & Manning, 2003].Barring the Women's Reservation case, politics was not the prime reason for delays or changes in most of the examples. Even where politics appears to be the reason, there is often more to it. While it is quite possible for purely political considerations to derail a well-structured policy-making process, in many cases *weaknesses in the policy-making process exacerbated political interference*. Indeed political "interference" was often (though by no means always) just a manifestation of factors ignored or missed in the policymaking process. Good policy-making structures and processes do matter and can overcome political bickering, as apparent from the evidence of other countries which are democracies. To cite one instance, a good part of the credit for the post-1945 Japanese economic miracle goes to the processes which enabled Japan to come out with coherent and well-implemented policies [Economic & Social Commission for Asia & The Pacific, 1995].

II. ATTRIBUTES OF A GOOD POLICY-MAKING PROCESS

It is interesting, and indeed revealing, that the literature on the public policymaking *process* is far less copious than the literature on *substantive* policy issues. The following section on the attributes of a good policy-making process draws on the literature, and on the authors' own experience in the policy making process.

A CONCEPTUAL OVERVIEW

One way of describing a "good" policy-making process is one that "is committed to producing a high quality decision—not any particular decision" and that "invests any decision made with a high degree of legitimacy, power and accuracy" [Moore, 1998]. What features or characteristics should a policymaking process have which, if present, would lead to high quality decisions?

First, to start with the most obvious, a good policy-making process would involve *due consideration of up-to-date available subject-matter knowledge and relevant data, and the use of available analytical tools*.

Second, policies made ostensibly for one sector often have significant impacts on other sectors: a transport policy (e.g. expansion of national highways in lieu of investment in rail) affects the environment; an environmental policy (stricter pollution norms) affects industrial development; a revenue enhancement measure intended to develop one sector can adversely affect another (e.g. the cess to fund the National Highway Development Project reduces the competitiveness of road transport). Policy-making therefore nearly always means trade-offs, the giving up of something to get something else, losses to one group or section in exchange for (hopefully larger) gains for another.

Policy-*making processes and structures should ensure the gathering of information on such inter-sectoral impacts, the analysis of trade-offs, and fully informed choices between alternatives after a proper consideration of effects on different sectors*. Many analytical techniques have been evolved to assist policy-makers in dealing with these issues, coming broadly under terms like policy analysis, program evaluation, cost-benefit analysis etc. These techniques are not without their critics, and their effect on policy–making has been less than their protagonists would like to think [Lindblom, 1990], [Lynn, 1978]. Nevertheless, these techniques are generally judged to have a positive effect on the quality of decisions made [Lynn, 1989].

Third, especially in a democratic polity, such *analysis should invariably include an assessment of the "winners" and "losers" from a given policy and a strategy for dealing with likely opposition from losers to what has been determined to be the "right" policy.*

Fourth, theory and practice both show that decisions which are seen to have 'legitimacy' are far more likely to be successfully implemented [Kliksberg, 2000]. Legitimacy is both procedural and substantive.

- Procedural legitimacy is sometimes narrowly viewed as meaning that the *decision is made by an authority legally authorised to make it*, but in practice *consultation of those affected is crucial to perceived legitimacy.* Procedural legitimacy can often be more important in securing the implementation of a policy, than its substantive merits.

- *Substantive legitimacy is achieved when the persons and groups who have knowledge and expertise in the field affected by a policy are involved in formulating the policy* [Moore,1998, pp.126-128].

Note that this point is about the legitimacy—not efficacy--of a policy. The question is not whether the policy was substantively correct, but whether persons who are publicly known or perceived to have subject matter knowledge were involved in making it.

Fifth, a good policy-making process should produce policies which can be executed swiftly and successfully. *This requires the close involvement, during formulation, of the persons who actually have to implement a policy on the ground*, [Darman, 1998] and implies a degree of 'decentralisation' of policymaking.

At the same time, a *degree of centralised control is necessary, so that the priorities and interests of implementers do not supplant the public interest.* Whether this central control should be confined to "process control" (i.e. control over how the decision is made) or should extend to "quality control"(control over the substance of the decision) is the subject of debate [Porter, 1980], but the choice is partly a factor of the kind of organisation and the kind of policy being made. On the whole, while policy-making must remain in touch with reality and be conscious of implementation issues, it should not be a prisoner of the current short-term priorities, time constraints and conveniences of implementers. A good policy making structure should, therefore, provide for appropriate separation between the policy and implementation functions

Finally, in order to make the (often difficult) decisions on trade-offs and make them without undue delay, information, analysis and good procedures alone are insufficient. *Those charged with making, or advising on, policy, must possess certain skills (e.g. in coordination, synthesis and integration) and attributes (such as freedom from bias)* which increase the likelihood of quick and sound decisions.

To recapitulate, a "good policy-making process" would meet the following criteria:-

1. the problems and issues confronting a sector are subjected to expert analysis;

2. information on overlaps and trade-offs with other sectors is systematically gathered and made available to policy-makers;

3. opposing points of view within and between sectors , are properly articulated, analysed and considered and those likely to benefited or harmed are identified and their reactions anticipated;

4. decisions are made with due legal authority, after consultation of those likely to be affected, and with the involvement of knowledgeable persons in the sector(s) concerned;

5. those responsible for implementation are systematically involved in the process, but are not allowed to take control of it;

6. policy-makers and /or their advisers have the honesty, independence, intellectual breadth and depth to properly consider and integrate multiple perspectives and help arrive at optimal policy choices within a reasonable time.

TRANSLATING THEORY INTO PRACTICE—MANAGING THE TRADE-OFFS

Unfortunately the application of these theoretical principles in designing a real-world structure is not simple. There are trade-offs. Criterion (i) – expert analysis of a given sector - is usually achieved by specialists in a field. The pursuit of specialised expertise often leads, quite logically, to fragmentation i.e. the creation of more and more specialised organisations--ministries, departments, directorates, etc. The narrower the specialisation, the greater the potential for depth in knowledge of that field. For example, instead of one Department of Science and Technology, one can have separate departments for Space, Ocean Development etc. Instead of an Education Department one can divide it into Primary Education, Secondary Education, Collegiate Education, Technical Education etc. In the years since Independence, the Central Government has created an ever-increasing number of more-specialised departments in place of more-generalised departments. (There are 82 departments in the Government of India today as against only 18 in 1948 [Report of the 5th Pay Commission, 1996].).

However, narrow specialisation diminishes knowledge of the larger picture, of overlaps and trade-offs. Thus, excessive pursuit of criterion (i) reduces the attainment of criterion (ii). Improved analysis may come at the cost of reduced synthesis — a weakness as prevalent in the private sector as in the public sector [Ackoff, 1999]. Besides, specialists in a real-world bureaucracy begin to acquire an interest in the pursuit of their specialism or ministry--expansion of that sector means more departments and hence more top jobs, faster promotion, greater responsibility, more prospects of public recognition etc. – thereby diminishing their independence and thus attainment of criteria (iii) (consideration of opposing points of view) and (vi) (independence and lack of bias).

Besides, while fragmentation improves specialised knowledge, it

- reduces communications between the fragmented units, both formal and informal, and
- reduces coordination and integration

21. Integration of different functions is intrinsically difficult and costly [Chambers,1974]. Officers in the same department interact frequently at meetings (formal communication) and may even meet daily for lunch (informal communication).

Disagreements between them may be quickly resolved by referral to their common superior. Officers in different departments interact less frequently and more formally, reducing the quantity and quality of information- and ideasharing. Thus as a corollary of the preceding criteria, a good policy-making structure must *neither be so wide as to militate against specialisation, nor be so fragmented as to affect integration* [Klitgaard, 1991]. What then is the 'right' or 'optimal' degree of fragmentation? In the following section, two general principles are suggested.

While policy in any sector can theoretically affect any other, in practice the number of interconnections is greatest among related sectors. Thus the interconnections or trade-offs between road transport and rail transport are greater than between road transport and space technology, while the interconnections between information technology and rail transport are less than between, say, information technology and telecommunications. This leads to the conclusion that:

As a general *principle, related sectors (meaning sectors with significant policy interactions between them) should be grouped together so as to maximise policy coordination.*

The lower down the hierarchy one operates, the greater the value of specialised knowledge. Thus the sanitary engineer operating a sewage pumping station needs very specific knowledge about the working of his pumps, a level of detail which his utility's chief executive does not need to know. By contrast, the chief executive has to have a basic level of awareness of every facet of the utility's operations. A heart surgeon in a teaching hospital needs highly specialised knowledge—but the Director of Medical Education needs a very different set of skills and information. The corollary is that,

As a general *principle, fragmentation needs to diminish as one goes higher up the hierarchy.*

Finally at the apex, namely the Prime Minister, one person becomes responsible for everything.

III. Weaknesses in India's Public Policy making

A comparison of the reality of policy-making in India with the theoretical framework outlined in the preceding section shows the following shortcomings.

Excessive Fragmentation in Thinking and Action

One of the main problems with policy-making in India, is extreme fragmentation in the structure. For example, the transport sector is dealt with by five departments/Ministries in the government of India whereas in the US and UK it is a part of one department (Department of Transport and Public Works in the US and Department of Environment, Transport and Regions in the UK). Similar examples exist in the energy, industry and social welfare sectors as well. Such fragmentation fails to recognize that actions taken in one sector have serious implications on another and may work at cross purposes with the policies of the other sector. Besides, it becomes very difficult, even for closely related sectors, to align their policies in accordance with a common overall agenda.

Excessive Overlap between Policy Making and Implementation

Another problem is the excessive overlap between implementation, program formulation and policy making which creates a tendency to focus on operational convenience rather than on public needs. Policy-making in Indian ministries occurs at the levels of Director and above, but the most important level (crucial for consideration of cross-cutting impacts) is that of the Secretaries to the Government of India, who are their Ministers' "policy advisers-in-chief". However, as mentioned earlier, the very same Secretaries spend a large part of their time bogged down on routine day-to-day administration of existing policy. Time is spent anticipating and answering parliamentary questions, attending meetings and functions on implementation issues etc. Partly the problem is symptomatic of over-centralisation—excessive concentration of implementation powers at the higher levels of the Ministries. Partly, it is also due to such officers being more comfortable with implementation matters than with policy making. The result is that sub-optimal policies, where adequate attention has not been paid to citizen needs, tend to emerge.

The following diagram attempts to depict both, the fragmented policy making structures in India and the low degree of separation between policy-making and implementation.

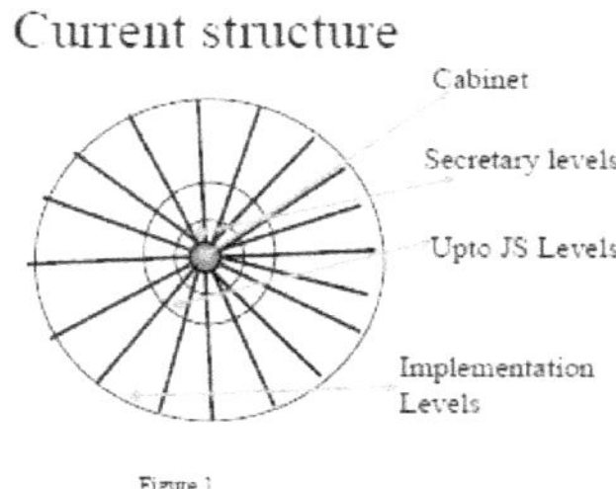

Note: JS denotes Joint Secretary (Joint Permanent Secretary)

In Figure 1, points nearer the centre of the circle represent higher levels of authority, the centre of the circle being the Cabinet. The black radii represent departmental divisions and their thickness denotes the relative lack of communication between departments. The two thin concentric circles denote the separation between implementation and policy making levels. They have been depicted as thin circles (as opposed to the thick radii) to signify that there is little effective separation between policy and implementation. The principle of gradual diminution in fragmentation as one goes up the hierarchy is not followed, a clear indicator that fragmentation at policy levels is excessive. (This is in contrast to the early years after Independence, when there were far fewer Secretaries.). Fragmentation has often occurred for reasons not directly connected with the design of an optimal structure. Indeed there is a widespread belief that fragmentation has been driven more by the compulsion to accommodate a larger council of ministers, in coalition politics, as well as the bureaucratic desire for more top level posts.

Recent experience suggests that inter-sectoral issues and trade-offs are becoming very difficult to address. The truck owners' strike of April 2003 is a   case in point: the road transport department had great difficulty dealing with the strike because many of the issues raised pertained to policy decisions of other ministries. Indeed the immediate triggers of the strike—diesel price increases, the mistaken apprehension of VAT on truckers' services—were totally beyond that department's purview. Yet the major impact of those decisions was on the road transport sector.

LACK OF NON-GOVERNMENTAL INPUTS AND INFORMED DEBATE

Often public policy is made without adequate input from outside government and without adequate debate on the issues involved. The best expertise in many sectors lies outside the Government. Yet the policy processes and structures of Government have no systematic means for obtaining outside inputs, for involving those affected by policies or for debating alternatives and their impacts on different groups. Most developed countries have a system of widespread public debate before a policy is approved. For example, in the US, the legislature subjects a new policy initiative to extensive debate not only in Committees but also in the Senate and House. Such debates not only enable an assessment of different viewpoints but also help build up a constituency in support of the policy through sound arguments. Probably the only example of fairly systematic consultation of outside expertise in India is in the process of formulating the Central Budget, where there is a long tradition of pre-budget confabulations with chosen members of industry, labour and academia.

There are several reasons for a poor pre-policy consultative process. *Firstly*, structures for consulting outsiders either do not exist or if they do, are moribund. *Secondly*, in the absence of good consultative structures, outsiders who do make themselves heard in the policy-making process are often single issue advocates. This makes them liable to the charge of having vested interests, and their views lose credibility. Even if a receptive civil servant were to take their views seriously, he would run the risk of appearing to do an illegitimate favour. *Thirdly*, outsiders involved in policy are usually allowed to make spasmodic or single issue inputs but are not required to sustain their interaction, to confront trade-offs or to meet the objections of other outsiders with opposite views. This makes it easy for outsiders who were indeed consulted, to then disclaim any responsibility for the final decision by protesting that their advice was only partially followed. *Fourthly* and as a result of the first three, there is a lack of identification of stakeholders with any policy. In countries like the USA, there are often strong advocates on both sides of a policy question—for example pro- and anti-abortion, pro- and anticapital punishment. In India, judging by the public reaction to many policy announcements, it would appear that almost every new policy announced by Government has "only opponents". This is because the 'winners' from a Government policy rarely feel involved in it, and hence rarely stand up and support it.

LACK OF SYSTEMATIC ANALYSIS AND INTEGRATION PRIOR TO POLICY-MAKING

Policy decisions are often made without adequate analysis of costs, benefits, trade-offs and consequences. There are several underlying causes for this:-

Excessive fragmentation: This has already been referred to. Fragmentation has led to a widespread prevalence of the 'blind men and the elephant' syndrome in policy-making.

Inadequate time spent on policy-making, mainly due to excessive overlap of policy-making and implementation and to overcentralisation of implementation authority (discussed above).

Inadequate professionalism of policy-makers and advisers: Debates have been common in India about the pros and cons of 'generalists' vs. 'specialists' in Government. There is a school of thought which suggests that the excessive involvement of poorly informed generalists is the main cause of poor policy-making and implementation. However, when it comes to the realm of policymaking and the making of trade-offs, experience in government and the private sector suggests that this is usually best handled by an intelligent, well-informed person who has a wide rather than narrow perspective. This person could be termed the "intelligent and informed generalist" who, though not a specialist in any one field, is in fact a specialist in analysis, integration and synthesis—i.e identifying problems, trade-offs and solutions. His strength and training lie in being well-informed about a variety of related subjects, in incisive analysis, and in intelligent use of information provided by specialists to frame policy options and assess their consequences.

Note that many successful businesses in India and abroad are headed by generalists (MBAs for instance) and the Tata conglomerate continues to operate through the generalist "Tata

Administrative Service" to man key positions—an approach regarded as a great success [Business Today, 2003]. The problem currently encountered is that the civil servants (who act as key policy advisers) often are not sufficiently well informed or trained to act in this manner. This could be described loosely but conveniently as "inadequate professionalism"

Inadequate consultation of in-house specialists: Even conceding that public policy-making might not be improved by insisting on specialists becoming the policy-makers, it is nevertheless crucial that specialist knowledge be fully consulted and utilised in arriving at policy. For reasons ranging from 'generalist arrogance' to interservice rivalries between groups of specialists, the available expertise of specialists within the Government is often under-utilised.

Mediocrity of in-house specialists: While there are many outstanding specialists working for the Government, there is a widespread feeling that many in-house specialists are not on top of their specialisms. This perception of mediocrity vis-à-vis outside experts tends to worsen the problem of inadequate consultation of even the good in-house specialists who get tarred with the same brush. It also promotes an undue respect for outside specialists and the error of accepting poorly formulated prescriptions from outsiders simply because they have a more professional or expert image.

REFORMING THE POLICY-MAKING PROCESS

The foregoing analysis attempted to identify the shortcomings in India's policy-making processes. This leads to the question: What can we do to improve policy-making?

The problems highlighted in the analysis can broadly be divided into two types. The first of these is structural—too much fragmentation, too much implementation work load on policy-makers, poor structure and process for involving outside experts and stakeholders. The second kind of problem lies with the competence of the people who man the structure—inadequate professionalism of the policy-making staff, and inadequate competence of the specialists. The next section of this paper makes specific reform suggestions on the first of these issues—institutional structures and processes. The second issue is dealt with in the following section. The feasibility of the proposals is considered in the final section.

IV. REFORMING INSTITUTIONAL STRUCTURES AND PROCESSES

This section of the paper proposes a set of reforms in institutional structures and processes. The proposed measures are grouped under three broad areas:-

- Reduction in fragmentation
- Separation of policy-making from implementation and de-centralising implementation authority
- Widening and enhancing the knowledge base used in policy-making and promoting integration and synthesis

REDUCTION IN FRAGMENTATION

It was observed that, *a priori*, there are both benefits and drawbacks from fragmentation. Broadly, the benefit is specialised knowledge while the demerit is weaker coordination and integration.

Having concluded that the present level of fragmentation is excessive, the question that arises is, how to go about reducing it. Applying the principles described earlier, the first reform would be to achieve a progressive decrease in fragmentation as one goes up the hierarchy. This would mean that fewer Secretaries, each of whom would handle more than one of the existing sectors.

The result would be that coordination and integration will be achieved far more smoothly. When deciding which portfolios to "broadband", the second principle-- the degree of interconnection and overlaps between sectors—would be the guide.

Figure 2 below is a schematic diagram of the proposed structure; Figure 1 (the existing structure) is repeated for ease of comparison.

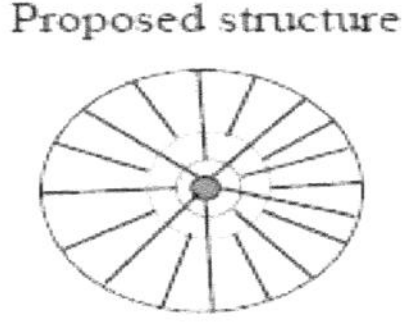

Figure 1 (repeated for ease of comparison)

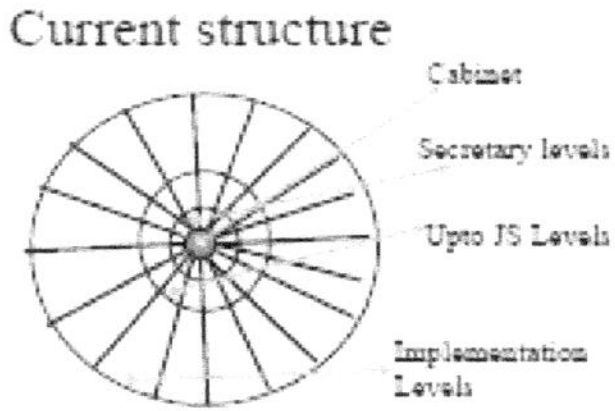

In Figure 2 at the higher levels of government, there is a progressive reduction in the number of "compartments"—denoted by *fewer radial lines.*

SEPARATING POLICY-MAKING FROM IMPLEMENTATION AND DECENTRALIZING IMPLEMENTATION AUTHORITY

The proposal to reduce fragmentation invites the question: How will the Secretaries cope with such enhanced responsibilities, when they are already overworked ?

It is true that senior level civil servants in the Government of India appear to be constantly overworked. But this is mainly because of:

- the heavy burden of day–to-day administrative (implementation) work, which occupies far more time than thinking on policy issues
- The high degree of centralisation of administrative powers.

The proposed reform is that the implementation responsibilities should be entrusted to Boards and Agencies, headed by a Director-General, in the rank of Joint Secretary or Additional Secretary. While his primary responsibility would be implementation, he would also provide essential inputs for policy making. He would, thus, be a bridge between policy and implementation. The Secretary will be responsible for policy-making and have no implementation responsibilities. He would only get feedback on the progress of implementation, largely to aid future policies or to correct existing policies. Files on individual implementation decisions will not go to the Secretary, nor will he attend meetings on implementation issues. This will not only release Secretaries from their excessive routine workload, but also give policy-making the focus it deserves. This change is depicted in Figure 2 : the thin lines separating policy and execution are replaced by thicker lines, denoting a much stronger separation of execution and policy-making.

However there are pitfalls in completely isolating the Secretary from implementation. The flow of information and policy-relevant ideas can be weakened if the policy-maker is not also the implementer. Secondly, lack of authority over current implementation can, in the real world, lead to a perception of diminished "power" with an attendant downgrading of the importance of the policy-making function. There is a way around this: the Director-General's annual performance appraisal should be carried out by the Secretary. This should ensure that the Secretary continues to have access to information and that the policy-making role is not seen as a secondary or unimportant one.

Such restructuring could pose a problem in accommodating a large council of ministers. For dealing with this, the Boards/ Agencies could have a political executive at the top, in the rank of Minister of State or Deputy Minister. Cabinet ministers may head policy-making broadband ministries. Accountability for policies would rest with the Cbinet Minister and for implementation with the Minister of State/Deputy Minister.

In fact, such separation of the policy advice function from the implementation or service delivery function has been a key ingredient of governance reforms in the UK, Australia, New Zealand [Commonwealth Secretariat, 1995a], Malaysia [Commonwealth Secretariat, 1995b] and other countries.

IMPROVING INTEGRATION AND THE FLOW OF KNOWLEDGE FROM OUTSIDE GOVERNMENT

The third broad reform would be to create structures which ensure the availability to policy-makers of non-Governmental inputs and subject matter expertise. To this end, each Ministry or Department should have a "Policy Advisory Group". This would consist of :

- Selected top civil servants, covering related sectors. To ensure that the groups do not become one more bureaucratic mechanism without clout, only Secretary-level officers should be on these groups.

- Stakeholder/ Industry representatives

- Academics with expertise in the field

These Policy Advisory Groups should cut across departmental viewpoints, and offer integrated policy suggestions. Consultation of the Policy Advisory Group and a consideration of the Group's views would be mandatory on all policy matters, before a proposal is placed before the Cabinet.

V. IMPROVING THE COMPETENCE AND SKILLS OF POLICY-MAKING MANPOWER

Earlier in this section, it was observed that policy-making is usually best supervised by the "informed and intelligent generalist". There is however a very big difference between a mere "generalist" and an "informed and intelligent generalist". Being "informed and intelligent" requires certain skills, namely the ability to

- structure a problem,

- assess what kinds of issues are likely to arise,

- know where to look for appropriate information and expert opinion,

- speak and understand the "language of the specialists" so as to communicate effectively with them and be able to interpret expert opinion.

Currently, the extent to which a generalist civil servant acquires these vital policy skills is left partly to the individual (his own efforts to acquire them) and partly to chance (the postings he holds). Despite sporadic efforts by the Department of Personnel to promote a degree of broad specialisation, little has actually been achieved.

The key reform which would greatly improve the policy-making competence of India's senior civil servants—and improve the competence of specialists in Government—is implementation of a well-designed career path which has strong incentives for the progressive acquisition of expertise and professional skills. Experience abroad, including in developing countries, shows this to be a significant contributor to good policy making.

The key requirement is the design of a career path which

- creates incentives to learn, and to acquire and apply the right skills

- strengthens links between academia and the administration

- identifies and weeds out poor performers

- ensures that only those with the requisite knowledge and intelligence make it to the top policy levels.

The following is an approach designed to achieve these results in the specific context of the Indian Administrative Service (IAS--the premier generalist civil service cadre in India, which accounts for the largest number of policy level positions):-

- All IAS officers should spend their first 10-12 years in general management, largely in field assignments. This will provide them with a thorough grounding in field realities and in basic managerial skills, which are crucial for making the right policy-choices.

- All officers would undergo an evaluation by an independent body. About 90% of the officers should be cleared for the next level with about 10% (relatively poor further promotion for a further 5-7 years before early retirement.

- Officers clearing the selection process would be assigned a broad specialisation, and undergo a specific training program leading up to a Masters and/or M.Phil Degree. The area of specialisation would be determined fairly and transparently based on educational background, demonstrated aptitude, performance in training programs, sectoral manpower needs, and individual preferences. An illustrative list of broad specialisms would be: economic and commercial management, financial management, personnel management, infrastructure management, Internal Security and Defence, Social sector management, Rural development and local administration, Health sector management, Education sector management, General management, regulatory matters and Governance.

- During the next 15 years, officers would work in their chosen broad specialism, and (if they desire) work towards a Ph.D, taking up spells of research in suitably timed sabbaticals.

- The academic qualifications acquired (M.Phil., Ph.D etc) would give academic endorsement and credit for an officer's achievements, provide a transparent and objective input for career progression, reduce complacency, inculcate a culture of continuous learning, and strengthen officers' self-confidence and ability to deal with peers in other countries and international institutions.

- Around the 27th year, they would, after a rigorous selection process, be assigned to a policy-making position. Selection would be done through the UPSC or another credible agency. This would be a substitute for the "empanelment" process. Only about 30% of the opening cohort should make it to this level. Those not selected will retire at the age of 55.

Similar career paths can be designed for other quasi-generalist services (like the Revenue Services, Accounts Services) and a suitably modified version for specialists (Economic Service, Engineering services, and scientific services).

The emphasis on academic qualifications in the proposed career path has the advantages that it would:-

- give academic endorsement and credit for an officer's achievements,
- provide a transparent and objective input for career progression,
- reduce complacency,
- inculcate a culture of continuous learning, and
- strengthen officers' self-confidence and ability to deal with peers in other countries and international institutions.

However, it also has some limitations and disadvantages. Mediocrity is widespread in Indian academia. This would reduce many of the theoretical advantages unless the choice of institutions was also tightly and centrally prescribed. The process of such prescription may well invite challenge from individuals or institutions left out. The skills required for academic success are not necessarily the same as those required for success in public management and public policy making; the services are replete with academically brilliant officers who are poor managers or policy-makers. There are also a few instances of superb administrators with just a Bachelor's degree. This limitation can be overcome by ensuring that academic achievement is only one factor in the selection process, but it does mean that the benefit of a 'transparent basis for career progression' is diminished to that degree. However, it also has some limitations and disadvantages. Mediocrity is widespread in Indian academia. This would reduce many of the theoretical advantages unless the choice of institutions was also tightly and centrally prescribed. The process of such prescription may well invite challenge from individuals or institutions left out.

The skills required for academic success are not necessarily the same as those required for success in public management and public policy making; the services are replete with academically brilliant officers who are poor managers or policy-makers. There are also a few instances of superb administrators with just a Bachelor's degree. This limitation can be overcome by ensuring that academic achievement is only one factor in the selection process, but it does mean that the benefit of a 'transparent basis for career progression' is diminished to that degree.

Unit V

PRINCIPAL MODELS FOR PUBLIC POLICY ANALYSIS

5.1. GENERAL CONSIDERATIONS

Policy analysis has been variously defined by scholars. For instance **Ukeles (1977:223)** defines it as:

The systematic investigation of the alternative policy options and the assembly and integration of the evidence for and against each option. It involves a problem solving approach, the collection and interpretation of information, and some attempt to predict the consequences of alternative courses of action.

Poster (1978:1) defines policy analysis as "analysis of the determinants, characteristic, and implications of public policies and programs and the substantive consequences and outcomes they produce". It is a set of techniques that seeks to answer the question of what the probable effects of a policy will be before they actually analysis as an activity that occurs before a policy comes into effect. But the fact remains that policy analysis can take place even when a policy has come into effect. However, a policy analysis undertaken on a program that is already in effect is more appropriately called a program evaluation.

For the purposes of this book, policy analysis is defined as a multidisciplinary and systematic investigation aimed at gathering and analyzing information about the likely consequences of public polices both before and after they occur. All policy analysis involve the application of systematic research techniques (drawn largely from the social sciences and based on measurements of program effectiveness, quality, cost, and impact) to the formulation, execution, and evaluation of public policy to create a more rational administrative system. Public policy analysis is aimed at improving the basis for public policy making. The fundamental purpose of policy analysis, according to **Beckman (1975)** is, "to facilitate the reading of sound policy decisions". Policy analysis also contributes to better policy implementation and performance through studies, determination of problems and the means to resolve them. Brewer and Deleon (1983:20) have developed the following processes of policy analysis:

THE PROCESS OF POLICY ANALYSIS

1. INITIATION

Initiation is the first stage in the process of policy analysis. It involves the conception of creative thoughts about a problem. This is further followed by the definition of objectives, designing of several innovative options, and then a tentative preliminary exploration of concepts, claims and possibilities.

2. ESTIMATION

This second stage involves a thorough investigation of concepts and claims, a scientific examination of impacts of continuing to do nothing as well as of each considered intervention option. Other issues involved under this stage include normative examination of likely consequences; development of program outlines; and establishment of expected performance criteria and indications.

3. SELECTION

The selection stage involves debating on possible options to be chosen; compromises, bargains, and accommodations; reduction of uncertainty about options; integration of ideological and other non-rational elements of decision; decisions among options; and assignment of executive responsibility.

4. IMPLEMENTATION

The fourth stage is the implementation stage. This is a crucial stage in the process, and involves development of rules, regulations, and guidelines to carry out decision. Another important aspect of this stage is the modification of decision to reflect operational constraints, including incentive and resources. This leads to the translation of decisions into operational terms, and finally the setting of program goals and standards, including schedule of operation.

5. EVALUATION

This stage in the process is concerned with the comparison of expected and actual performance levels according to established criteria, as well as the assignment of responsibility for discovered discrepancies in performance.

6. TERMINATION

This is the final stage in the process of policy analysis. The focus at this stage is the determination of costs, consequences, and benefits for reductions or closures.

The core decision in economics is "What do we want and what can we get?. Ordinarily we want more than we can get, and because our capabilities are limited and the resources available to us scarce, choices must be made among our competing desires. The Port Authority would like to expand airport operations and at the same time reduce noise levels. It cannot do both; as headlines testify, the choice is difficult. How choices should be made-the whole problem of allocating scarce resources among competing ends-is the stuff of economics and the subject of this book. [36]

In public policy analysis we focus on choices in the public sector, on how decisions should be made by governments at all levels and by nonprofit institutions. As we are by now all well aware, the government is not a business, and in many respects it cannot be run like a business. Its goals are different and it operates under different constraints. Yet the basic elements of good decisions are the same in all arenas, and the methods for making them set forth here are applicable for all decision makers, public and private.

Our starting point is a fundamental model of choice. We have seen that a model is a simplified representation of some aspect of the real world, a deliberate distillation of reality to extract the essential features of a situation. The fundamental choice model is particularly valuable because it offers a universal yet succinct way of looking at problems in terms of the two primary elements of any act of choice: [37]

- The alternatives available to the decision maker; and
- His preferences among these alternatives.

The model forces the decision maker to express the alternatives he faces and his preferences among them in comparable units. You will see from our examples that the alternatives may sometimes be described in tangible terms, actual outputs that can be seen and counted, such as electricity and water, or allergy tests and electrocardiograms. At other times the outputs of the alternative choices will be described in terms of intangible attributes such as intelligence and beauty, or taste and nutrition, or safety and speed. Some of these intangibles can be measured more or less objectively; others cannot. The model is flexible; it easily handles all types of attributes, whether described by hard numbers or paragraphs of prose, so long as the decision maker's preferences are expressed in the same terms as the alternatives.[38]

In terms of alternatives available to the decision maker, the first element of the basic model describes the alternatives available to the decision maker. If this were a standard economics text, we would introduce you to apples and oranges and ask you to consider the plight of the grocery shopper who must allocate his fruit budget between those two goods. But this is a document about public decisions, so we ask you instead to play the part of a public official who must choose among several alternative dam projects. These projects are identical in every respect-costs, environmental consequences, and so on-except two: they produce different amounts of electric power and water for irrigation. In other words, the decision maker faces a certain number of alternative quantities of power and water. [39]

A main general concept about public policy analysis is the marginal analysis tool. This concept includes the discussion of marginal rates of transformation and substitution is only one example of the type of analysis that forms the core of traditional microeconomics theory. In a nutshell, in order to achieve an optimal result, the allocation of scarce resources among competing uses must satisfy certain marginal equalities. For example, the consumer should allocate his budget so that he gets the same satisfaction from the last dollar he spends on orange juice and the last dollar he spends on going to the ballet. And a rational consumer will do just that, even though he will rarely do so consciously. A farmer or the manager of a pencil factory should expand production just to the point where his last dollar of sales costs him exactly \$1. Producing more diminishes his profit, producing less means that he forgoes some of the profit he might have reaped. Similarly, a public decision maker-a mayor, for example should allocate spending on park maintenance and on fire protection so that the last dollar spent on each is equally satisfying to the society he represents. [40]

The model of choice to develop public policy analysis requires that preferences be expressed in the same units as the outcomes of the various alternatives proposed. Thus, if the decision maker is offered a choice among assorted combinations of apples and oranges, his preferences must be expressed also in terms of apples and oranges. Conversely, if he is to choose a mix of strange fruit whose attributes are a mystery to him, although he knows his preferences for, say, vitamins and juiciness, the outcomes of the various possible choices must be expressed not as bundles of fruit but as combinations of these attributes. In other words, he must be able to measure these fruits in terms of the characteristics he understands, cares about, and can work with.[41]

The following sections will address discussions concerning the most frequently models used to carry out public policy analysis.

5.2. Difference Equations

This method is more useful when the features of the phenomenon under study are quantitative variables. Difference equations have the significant advantage to allow us to take into account the dynamic change in the variables, and thus the possibility to identify possible trends of the variables.

5.2.1. A General Description and Illustrations

There are two ways we can represent dynamic processes. We can view things as changing continuously over time, which is in fact generally the case, or we can break in on a process or system at specified time intervals and see where things are.

Difference equations take the period-by-period or discrete approach: they relate the value of a variable in a given time period to its values in periods past. They are an essential feature of the financial world; indeed the compound interest model that we used is a simple difference equation:

$$S_1 = (1 + r) \, S_0$$

Here S1, the sum of money in a savings bank account at the end of a year, is related to the initial sum So; r is the rate of interest. For example, this equation is valid whether r is 5 percent, 7 percent, or 100 percent. Note the use of subscripts, numbers or letters written to the right of and a little below the symbol for the variable, to indicate the specific time at which a variable is being valued. They are typical of difference equations: using the variables So and S1 rather than completely different symbols such as A and B for the variables serves to remind us that we are talking about a particular chunk of money, even though the exact sum in question is different at different times. [42]

Listed below are a few illustrations of the many sorts of situations in which difference equation models are useful:

1. A couple wishes to set aside money to supplement Social Security when they retire in twenty years. They want to know what their savings will be when they retire if they invest $2000 per year at 7 percent interest, and how long those savings will last if after retirement they withdraw $5000 per year, continuing to earn 7 percent on the balance left in their account.

2. A school district has overcrowded classrooms. There is pressure to relieve this overcrowding, either by building a new school or by renting temporary facilities. In order to decide between these two alternatives, the school board needs projections of the school-age population in the district over the next two decades.

3. The president of a university is concerned about its ability to fund ongoing programs. He needs projections of income and expenses over the next 10 years to help him decide what policies to follow with respect to tuition, scholarship aid, and faculty hiring.

4. A state department of public health is considering a new program to detect and treat hypertensives. It has guesstimates of how many new hypertensives would be discovered every month, what proportion would then enter treatment, and what the attrition rate from the program would be. In order to put together a budget, the department needs estimates of the number of people in treatment during the first two years of the program.

5. The 1970 Clear Air Act mandates stepped reduction in the permissible level of pollutants emitted by new cars. The possibility of requiring the owners of older cars to add pollution control devices has been discussed. Given the rates at which older cars go out of service, how much difference would such a policy make in the total amount of auto emissions?

6.   A mosquito control district is considering several alternative spraying programs, all of which have the same dollar cost. It needs a model of mosquito reproduction and of the effects of different spraying programs in order to determine the most effective plan. [43]

An extremely important aspect of difference equations is the choice of the appropriate time interval-the amount of time that elapses between time 0 and time 1-to use in a difference equation depends on the particular problem at hand. If we were examining the growth of a flu epidemic, for instance, days or weeks might be appropriate, whereas for the growth of world population we would be more likely to look at years or decades.[44]

5.2.2. THE GENERAL FORM OF A DIFFERENCE EQUATION

Thus far our difference equations have modeled changes for specific periods of time, an initial period (0) and one period later (1). Usually we are more interested in a general statement that relates the value of the variable in any time period to its value in the preceding period. In the compound interest model, it would be useful to have an expression for Sn, the sum at the nth period, in terms of what S was in period (n-1). This of course offers greater flexibility in applying the formula. In this case it is clear what that formula must be; we simply write:

$$S_n = (1 + r)\, S_{n-1}$$

For all $n^3\ 1$

Where Sn-1 is the sum on deposit at the end of the (n-1) period. This equation is called the general form of the difference equation, because it holds in general and not just for specific values of n. It is a first-order difference equation because the variable Sn can be determined from its value in the one preceding period only. [45]

5.2.3. DIFFERENCE EQUATIONS OF HIGHER ORDER

Consider the following statement:

The Bonex Company prefers, earnings permitting, to pay dividends according to the following rule: The dividend on a share of common stock should be equal to 90 percent of last year's dividend plus one and one-half times the previous year's change in dividend.

This exercise is designed to illustrate a situation slightly more complicated than those previously encountered. Here we are concerned with a dividend, D, that depends on its value not only in the last period but also in the period before last. The general difference equation is:

$$Dn = .90Dn\text{-}1 + 1.5(Dn\text{-}1 - Dn\text{-}2) = 2.4Dn\text{-}1 - 1.5Dn\text{-}2, \ n>=2$$

This is presented only as an example, the difference equations in this case is of higher order, since the value of n must be equal or higher than 2.[46]

5.2.4. THE USE OF DIFFERENCE EQUATIONS IN MODELING

Ordinarily we expect to see difference equations used as sub models, to predict parts of a system rather than the system as a whole. This is not to downgrade the importance of difference equations. Indeed, few people would view predictions about the future availability of oil as unimportant. In constructing their models, policy analysts rely on the existing age structure and predictions as to the future behavior of variables such as age-specific birth rates, death rates, migration rates, percent of the population gainfully employed, retirement age, wage rates, and the like, with difference equations playing a central role.

In this part we have discussed the use of difference equations primarily as a vehicle for introducing a variety of concepts and techniques. We must keep in mind that our main goal in developing these models is better predictions of the outcomes of policy alternatives.[47]

5.3. QUEUING OR RANKING METHOD

5.3.1. GENERAL FEATURES

Problems of public policy analysis in which it is possible to apply queuing or ranking methods, are characterized by the fact that a service facility is too limited to provide instantaneous service to all of its customers on all occasions. We do not want that people wait for services, but on the other hand, installing additional service capacity is too expensive. Queuing problems arise whenever a service facility is too limited to provide instantaneous service to all of its customers on all occasions. When the customers arrive more swiftly than they can be serviced, lines or queues will develop. Waiting is costly; frequently we would pay to avoid it.

It is, of course, impossible to eliminate waiting altogether; the costs would be prohibitive. A fire engine for every house in a rural area would protect against the one in a trillion possibility that all the engines will be needed at the same time, but it would obviously be undesirable. This is a straightforward matter of tradeoffs: the shorter we wish waiting time to be, the more facilities we must have available. To be more specific, the model can tell us how the waiting time for service will respond to the level of facilities that is made available. How much, for example, can the local Social Security office shorten clients' waiting times by opening another window? Occasionally it is also possible to change the time required for service; what would be the result of improving procedures so as to cut service time by two minutes?[48]

Studying the way queues behave is important for public policy because the relationship between waiting times and service capacity is far from obvious, while the cost of providing extra capacity is likely to be large. Even simple models can help us grasp the essence of a great variety of real-world situations, and the results are often surprising.

5.3.2. PROBABILISTIC QUEUING MODELS

When customers arrive for service at a regular and predictable rate, as we assumed they did at the toll bridge, long lines may develop as a result of sheer numbers; expected arrivals may exceed the service capacity. A deterministic model that pays no attention to uncertainties can then predict directly the effects of adding or subtracting stations. Most queuing problems are not so tractable; customers usually arrive at irregular rates. Take the case of a facility that can serve up to 12 people per hour if they arrive at regular intervals. One day 3 people may arrive during the first hour and 18 during the next hour. As a result, people must queue up even when there is, on average, enough service capacity. In other words, a facility may be able on paper to serve a given number of customers per day provided they arrive regularly. But if they arrive irregularly, as a practical matter the facility will serve far fewer than its theoretical capacity. As the average number demanding service each day rises, waiting times will become intolerable.

In the real world, queuing systems are of course likely to be much more complex and to involve several different kinds of random events. In principle the problem is still likely to be straightforward, although programming the computer may become more of a chore. It's useful to keep in mind a checklist of the types of random events and complications that can occur in a queuing system. These fall under three main aspects:[49]

1. Arrivals. Arrival intervals may be independent of one another, or the fact of one arrival may influence the probability as to when the next occurs. The latter will true whenever customers are likely to arrive in groups, as at an airport customs station. The arrivals in the Registry of Motor Vehicles example were independent, on the assumption that a driver's license expires on the holder's birthday. In contrast, 20 percent of the hypertension clinic patients arrived in groups of two or more, reflecting the greater likelihood that people would choose to make joint trips to the facility. It is also possible that the arrival pattern might vary with the time of day, or with the number of people waiting for service.[50] So if we wished to make the model more sophisticated, we could relate patient arrival frequencies to the number of patients waiting. We might, for example, use one frequency distribution when fewer than 5 people are waiting, another when 5 to 10 are waiting, and so on. In this way we would recognize the influence of service characteristics on arrival behavior. It's more work to program the computer for the fancier model, but conceptually the problem is no more difficult.

2. Service times. Different people may require different service times. Further, the service time for on person may be affected by the number waiting of by the nature of the services rendered those who preceded him. Again, such variations on the basic model make the programming more burdensome, and it would be necessary to develop data on the frequency distribution for service times. But no fundamental changes in the model are required.

3. The "queue discipline." The way in which the queue forms and moves may not be a straightforward one right after the other straight line process. There may be more than one line; line jumping may be permitted; perhaps people who receive service must then get in another queue for a second service. With the hypertension clinic's lunch breaks, we introduced the possibility of a variable number of service stations. There may be bumping or other priority procedures.

Note that changes in the quality of service will show up as changes in queuing behavior only if arrival or service times of the queue discipline are affected. Service quality as such need not appear independently in the model.

5.4. SIMULATION AND NON-LINEAL METHODS

5.4.1. GENERAL FEATURES

The policy arena, the true world of affairs, is not always compatible to the straightforward use of analytic methods. The analyst may be confronted with problems that are too intricate to solve directly. He can write down equations that describe the workings of a system, and this may be a useful discipline in itself. But given the complex interactions within the system, even modern mathematical techniques are not powerful enough to predict the consequences of any policy choice.

In such a case, we can try to construct a laboratory model of the system. The model can be physical; frequently ship or plane designs are tested on scale models in water tanks or wind tunnels. It may be highly abstract; military strategies are sometimes tested by reproducing battlefield conditions on what is essentially a game board. If alternative predictions are made as to how individual encounters between elements of the opposing forces will be resolved, the board representation enables army strategists to consider the overall outcome of many simultaneous encounters. [51]

Models of this sort are also helpful to transportation planners who must predict traffic flows, say to determine the benefits of a new bypass. Behavioral equations are employed to predict , for instance, how motorists' decisions will respond to traffic density-how they will change the timing of their trips, or the routes, or the destinations. A simulation method thus attempts to reproduce a system in what is the equivalent of a laboratory setting, in many occasions we need to conclude using concepts of chaos theory in order to represent the main factors, the more important limitations concerning the phenomenon under study, and the more probable trends of results.

Sometimes we wish to examine the histories that may result from alternative policy choices. For example, suppose a number of different pollutants are discharged into a river at several places along it. A model can be constructed to relate water conditions at various points downstream to the levels of these discharges. This model of the river basin could then be used for studying the effects of regulatory discharge levels. Any number of policy choices in the form of possible combinations of discharge levels may be investigated, and their performance assessed.

At other times we wish to investigate the implications of changes in certain key parameters. A river, for example, has an extraordinary ability to cleanse itself-provided pollution does not exceed certain levels. Even though it is polluted over an upstream stretch, the river may be relatively free of pollution at its mouth. Perhaps the volume of municipal sewage discharges is critical for this regenerative capacity. [52]

Simulations directed to random situations, such as those usually encountered in queuing problems, generally run through a great number of histories to provide a feel for the frequency distribution of outcomes.

5.4.2. MACROECONOMIC SIMULATION

In the last quarter century, simulations of national economies and of the world economy have come into increasing prominence. These models use large numbers of data to predict the behavior of key variables in the economy-investment, consumption, employment, imports and exports, government expenditures, and the like-over the next few quarters or years. A typical model might relate consumption in year t, for example, to wages and profits in the same year, and investment in year t to profits in years t and (t-1). Government economists trying to determine the optimal level of government spending and corporate planners trying to determine the optimal level of investment rely on them. To a degree, the models build in an element of self-fulfillment as decision makers respond to their predictions. Similar macroeconomic models are now used to try to predict future world use of certain vital resources, especially oil. [53]

5.4.3. SIMULATION AS AN ANALYTIC TOOL

Analysts recognize that there are many problems in formulating informative simulations and usually employ them only as a last resort. The difficulties encountered in building the model can be formidable; frequently independent verification of the accuracy of the model is impossible. In addition, probabilistic output, the usual output of a simulation, is susceptible to misuse, particularly if some of the information is not presented.

For example, suppose the average epidemic for a population of 100 people turns out to be 5 cases. This average could have resulted from epidemic sizes of 4, 7, 3, 5, 6, and so on, year after year. Or it could conceivably conceal the fact that no epidemic occurs 19 years out of 20, but then everyone is laid low at once; the average epidemic is still 5 cases. Obviously this information could be misleading; as a precaution, the analyst should insist on seeing a sampling of complete runs as well as the final averages. Despite these risks, in many situations informative simulation is the appropriate recourse for the analyst. Used wisely, it is an indispensable tool for predicting the outcomes of alternative policies.[54]

5.5. MARKOV CHAINS

Simple models sometimes yield compelling conclusions. Such models are worthy of study if their basic elements reappear in a variety of situations. Markov models are among these models; an understanding of them yields insights into a number of policy issues. Pollutants moving through the biosphere, mentally ill individuals moving from one level of functional capability to another, heroin users moving from addiction to treatment to abstention and back again-all can be illuminated by casting them in a Markov framework.

Consider the following situation, [55] which we will describe with the aid of a Markov model. New Kent has a labor force of 10,000 people. In any month, each of these 10,000 people is either employed (E) or unemployed (U). At present, 3000 are unemployed. As things now stand, 90 percent of those employed in one y ear are still employed the following year, while 40 percent of the unemployed find jobs and are employed in the next year. These proportions hold true year after year. New Kent's employment situation is summarized in the following table or matrix. This type of matrix is called a transition matrix because it describes how changes take place from one period to another.

Next period

	E	U
E	.90	.10

This period

U	.40	.60

E = employed

U = unemployed

The first row of numbers tells us what proportion of the people who are employed in the first period will still be employed in the next, and what proportion will be unemployed. Thus the .90 in row E, column E. means that of the people who are employed in the first period, .90 or 90 percent will be employed in the next period. The second row gives us the same information about those who are unemployed in the first period. We might also have labeled the two periods "y" and "y+1," since it is stipulated that the proportions don't change from year to year.

We could have used a set of difference equations to set forth the information contained in the transition matrix:

$$E2 = .90E1 + .40U1$$
$$U2 = .10E1 + .60U1$$

The main advantage of the matrix notation is its simplicity, in writing and especially in manipulation. This becomes much more important as the number of different categories increases.

The situation we have just examined is an example of a Markov system. In this case we have considered movements within an entire population, New Kent's labor force, from employed or unemployed in one period to employed or unemployed in the next period. When we observe the probabilistic movements of a single individual, the process is called a Markov chain. The arithmetic for the two situation is identical.[56]

5.5.1. MARKOV CHAINS: AN EXAMPLE

Let's consider an individual-we'll call him Smith-who is either well (W) or sick (S). Moreover, if Smith is well one day, he has an 80 percent chance of being well the next day. If he is sick, he has a 50 percent chance of being well the next day. These probabilities depend only on his condition today, an assumption that is crucial; his previous history doesn't matter. Smith's health is completely described by the following transition matrix, which defines a Markov chain:

Period 2

		W	S
	W	.80	.20
Period 1			
	S	.50	.50

Customarily we assign a label, let us call it P, to this matrix and write it simply as

$$P = \begin{matrix} .8 & .2 \\ .5 & .5 \end{matrix}$$

These probabilities for the state of Smith's health hold for any two consecutive periods.[57]

5.5.2. MAIN PROPERTIES OF A TRANSITION MATRIX

The main properties of a transition matrix that define a finite Markov chain, taking into account the aforementioned example are:

First, there must be a finite number of well-defined categories or states, such that the individual falls in one and only one state in each period; the mathematician's phrase is mutually exclusive and collectively exhaustive. This means that the system is closed-the individual always stays within it and does not move to some state outside the system, which is equivalent to stating that the numbers in each row of the matrix must add up to 1. Sometimes this inclusiveness requirement may be satisfied by enlarging the matrix, in other words by adding states so that all possibilities are accounted for. For example, suppose Smith, when he is well, has an 80 percent chance of remaining well and a 15 percent chance or being sick in the following period. He also has a 5 percent chance of dying and hence moving out of the two-state system. We may keep him in the system by adding "dead" as a third state.

A second property is that the probabilities in the transition matrix must be the same for any tow consecutive periods.

A third property is the so-called Markov condition: the probabilities must have no memory. It doesn't matter whether Smith was well or sick yesterday; the probability of his being well tomorrow depends only on how he is today. Suppose you find that the probability of his being well tomorrow, given that he is sick today, depends on how long he has been sick, and not just on whether he's well or sick in this period. Perhaps that probability is 50 percent if he has been sick one day, but only 30 percent if he has been sick longer. At first glance this presents insurmountable difficulties, but if only a few periods of history matter we can cope with the situation. In this particular set of circumstances, we replace the state "sick" with two states, "sick for one day" (S1) and "sick for two days or longer" (S2). The matrix Q would then represent a Markov chain:

Period 2

		W	S1	S2		
	W	.80	.20	0		
Period 1	S1	.50	0	.50	=	Q
	S2	.30	0	.70		

W = well

S1 = sick for one day

S2 = sick for two days or longer

If the number of states that the chain "remembers" is finite, it is possible to satisfy the Markov requirement by redefining the states in this manner.

A fourth property of a Markov chain is that time periods must be uniform in length. This may seem to be a superfluous requirement , as here they are automatically defined that way. But now and then it can give trouble. Generations, for example, are a very difficult time unit to work with. Moreover, with longer periods we have to pay attention to moves out of and back into a state within a single period. If these conditions-inclusive states, constant and memory-less probabilities, and uniform period lengths-are satisfied, then we have a Markov chain.[58]

5.5.3. Regular, Absorbing, and Cyclical Chains

With regular Markov chains we may draw two conclusions about the long-run probabilities: (1) for the long run, the probability of being in a particular state approaches an equilibrium value that is independent of the state that the individual is in initially; (2) these equilibrium probabilities may be interpreted as the percent of time spent in each state over the very long run.

With absorbing chains, the equilibrium is frequently uninteresting. We are more likely to want to know how many periods an individual can be expected to spend in each state before he is absorbed, or how quickly he is likely to get trapped. If there is more than one absorbing state, we may be interested in knowing what the probability is that the individual lands in each.

The fully cyclical chains tell us no more than what is intuitively obvious. The rotation continues perpetually, and where you are at any particular time depends on where you started and how many periods have passed. with a partially cyclical chain, the individual will become trapped in the rotation eventually, but if we know where he started, we will at least be able to estimate the expected number of periods that will pass before he is caught up in the rotation.

Finally, it is important to specify how the long run is in term of Markov chains. The answer is, "It all depends." If there is very little movement between states and if there are a large number of states, the system will be slow to converge toward its equilibrium probabilities. For example, consider the following well-sick transition matrix:

Period 2

		W	S
	W	.99999	.00001
Period 1			
	S	.00003	.99997

W = well

S = sick

The equilibrium probabilities for this system are .75 and .25 for well and sick. But this is scant comfort for a sick man, whose chances of getting well quickly are slim. Contrast this with our earlier well-sick matrix, where the long-run probabilities weren't quite as favorable (.714 and .286), but which converged to the equilibrium probabilities much more rapidly. If there are a large number of states, rather than just two, and period length is , say, one week, the system may take years to come close to equilibrium.[59]

5.6. COST-BENEFIT METHOD

Benefit-cost analysis is one of the principal analytical framework used to evaluate public expenditure decisions. This approach requires systematic enumeration of all benefits and all costs, tangible and intangible, whether readily quantifiable or difficult to measure, that will affect to all members of society if a particular project is adopted.

Benefit-cost analysis is sometimes described as the public household's version of a profit and loss statement. The analogy is strained; benefit-cost analysis examines all impacts of a project, internal and external, whereas a private business is presumed to look only at those that affect its own welfare, that its cost-benefit analysis must take into consideration externalities of a program, project, action or activity. [60]

The rationale for benefit-cost analysis is economic efficiency; it aims to ensure that resources are put to their most valuable use, including the significant possibility of leaving them in private hands. As a practical matter, benefit-cost analysis is most helpful in assessing well-defined projects. It would be of great assistance in choosing among alternative pollution-control systems for a particular river system, or in deciding whether road repairs in a community should be made with a new, more weather-resistant asphalt.

5.6.1. COST-BENEFIT ANALYSIS AND PROJECT EVALUATIONS

For many analysts the core approach to benefit-cost analysis is positive and enthusiastic. But it would be unfair to praise the merits of project evaluation techniques without identifying their liabilities as well. Benefit-cost analysis is especially vulnerable to misapplication through carelessness, naiveté, or outright deception. The techniques are potentially dangerous to the extent that they convey an aura of precision and objectivity. Logically they can be no more precise than the assumptions and valuations that they employ; frequently, through the compounding of error, they may be less so. Deception is quite a different matter, involving submerged assumptions, unfairly chosen valuations, and purposeful misestimates. [61]

Bureaucratic agencies, for example, have powerful incentives to underestimate the costs of proposed projects. Any procedure for making policy choices, from divine guidance to computer algorithms, can be manipulated unfairly. Since project evaluation techniques have been widely used in the past, it is no surprise that they have also been misapplied in some circumstances. But they are also somewhat less susceptible to manipulation than the more informal approaches to decision making, for they are designed to highlight the ingredients that go into a choice. If presented in a professional manner, they lend themselves to the introduction of alternative sets of assumptions that enable the policy maker and his critics to see whether different conclusions would emerge. Thus an important contribution of benefit-cost analysis is the information it provides to the political process.

Project evaluation techniques have proven themselves in a variety of arenas. Recently, benefit-cost and cost-effectiveness studies have been applied to a wide range of medical procedures, helping doctors to determine, for example, which patients should be routinely screened for hypertension and how they should be treated.

5.6.2. THE PROCEDURE

In principle, the procedure followed in a benefit-cost analysis consists of five steps.

- The project or projects to be analyzed are identified.

- All the impacts, both favorable and unfavorable, present and future, on all of society are determined.

- Values, usually in dollars, are assigned to these impacts. Favorable impacts will be registered as benefits, unfavorable ones as costs.

- The net benefit (total benefit minus total cost) is calculated.

- The choice is made. Criteria for making this decision are discussed in a later section of this chapter.

Benefit-cost analysis is a tool, indeed a most sophisticated set of tools. The mechanical elements of benefit-cost analysis are decision rules to determine whether a project or projects should be undertaken, and if so at what scale of activity. These decision rules do not spring into existence by some magical process; rather they are carefully designed to ensure that public decisions accurately reflect what it is that the society wants to accomplish. [62]

The formal rules for benefit-cost analysis use as inputs estimates of the benefits and costs of the projects. But a knowledge of these rules is only the beginning of wisdom for the decision maker. He must confront such matters as:

1. Deciding which rule is appropriate for use in any particular circumstance;
2. Placing a complex problem in a benefit-cost framework;
3. Computing estimates of benefits and costs; and
4. Deciding at what level of detail and sophistication an analysis should be conducted.

5.7. LINEAR PROGRAMMING

Of the various types of operations research, mathematical programming, and linear programming in particular, is the most highly developed and widely used. Programming is a means of optimizing; i.e., it is concerned with choosing the best levels for various activities in situations where these activities compete for scarce resources, or with choosing the minimum-cost method of producing required outputs.

There are situations where mathematical programming, whether used as a formal technique or as a guide to thinking, is enormously helpful. In some cases it can give us an outright solution, say an assignment of the police officers. In others it offers a solution only if we are able to make certain value judgments; perhaps we can assign weights to the cases the legal aid office might handle. At still other times no immediate answers are forthcoming, but greater insights may be gained by trying to structure the problem in a programming format by thinking carefully about the limited inputs available, the outputs desired, and the relationships among them. With such a problem we are still a long way from a decision, but at least we are asking better questions. [63]

5.7.1. THE ELEMENTS OF A LINEAR PROGRAMMING PROBLEM

The linear case assumes, first, that all relations between variables are proportional. If we double the inputs, we will double the outputs as well. Thus, if we need 1 widget and 2 gadgets to make 1 bobbin, we will need 2 widgets and 4 gadgets to make 2 bobbins. Economists refer to his property as "constant returns to scale." Second, we assume that all variable inputs and all outputs are infinitely divisible: fractional bobbins and gadgets cause us no problems. Third, we also assume that processes can be added together.

Anyone who understands linear programming can readily comprehend the basic ideas behind the more complicated types of mathematical programming. Our assumptions of constant returns, divisibility, and additivity are purely for expository reasons; none is critical for the kind of use that we wish to make of mathematical programming.

Political, economic, social, and institutional constraints usually place direct limits on levels at which the activities may be used. For example, in the diet problem we might wish to achieve a taste balance as well as a nutritional balance. A typical set of budget constraints for an institution might require that no program receive less than last year, nor more than a 10 percent increase over last year. Or it might specify that the ratio of the amounts expended on two programs remain within certain limits. In all these cases we are, in a sense, establishing subsidiary objectives for certain activities.

5.7.2. THE LIMITATIONS OF LINEAR PROGRAMMING

First, some of the relationships may be nonlinear, and some of the variables may take only integral values.[64]

Second, the constraints are such that no feasible solution yields acceptable score on the objective function. In that case, one possibility is merely too do the best we can with the onerous set of constraints. Alternatively, we can go back and see if the original problem can be re specified. Perhaps when the lack of acceptability of outcomes is pointed out to the individuals or agencies that imposed the constraints.

Unit VI

PUBLIC POLICY ANALYSIS: A GENERAL METHODOLOGY TO APPLY

The public decision maker has a difficult task. He confronts all the problems of an individual choosing for himself and, because he is acting on behalf of others, many additional problems as well. The environment in which he makes his choices is restricted in a multitude of ways. Resources-whether tax dollars, available space, or talented personnel-are scarce, and their effective allocation may be constrained by political considerations or the limited capabilities of sluggish bureaucracies. Nevertheless, the essence of the public decision problem is that described in the model of choice. There we shoed, with the aid of a simple diagram, how effective choices can be made when two essential ingredients can be identified: (1) the alternatives that are available, including a description of the attributes, and (2) the decision maker's preferences among alternative combinations of those attributes. General steps to apply the methodology for public analysis is presented here. [65]

6.1.   ESTABLISHING THE CONTEXT

Usually the most frequently questions asked are: What is the underlying problem that must be dealt with? When contemplating action in any policy area, the first step is to determine whether and why there is a problem at all. In a market-oriented society, the question becomes: Is the market performing satisfactorily in this area, and if not, why not?

Considering the context and in social and economic terms, the range of possible explanations for unsatisfactory market performance are:

1.   Information is not shared costlessly among all prospective participants in the market.
2.   Transactions costs significantly impede the conduct of beneficial trades.
3.   The relevant markets do not exist.
4.   Some of the participants in the market exercise market power.
5.   Externalities are present, so that the actions of one individual (whether a person or an organization) affect the welfare of another.
6.   The commodity involved in the policy choice is a public good.

Under any of these conditions, or if a compelling distributional objective will be served, government intervention may be appropriate. A policy analysis is then merited. [66]

6.2. DETERMINING ALTERNATIVES

With the context of the problem clearly in mind, we can proceed to the second step: What are the alternative courses of action? The alternatives for policy choice are often much broader than they first seem. Government intervention can take many forms; in any particular situation it is important to determine which type is most appropriate.

Can the alternative courses of action be designed so as to take advantage of additional information as it becomes available? A flexible decision process will enable the decision maker to change his course of action as he learns more about the real world in which he must operate. [67]

6.3. Establishing the Consequences

Once the problem is well-defined and the alternative courses of action delineated, the policy analyst must try to predict what will happen. What are the consequences of each of the alternative actions? Occasionally, mere reflection will be sufficient to trace the course from actions to outcomes. In some situations, the model will serve as little more than an intellectual guide.

Especially in this point we need to keep in mind the political and social role of actors and institutions. Since the public policy analysis is going to be useful as a tool, to produce results, the repercussions in form of predictable scenarios are crucial to consider. In this aspect the consideration of non lineal models are indispensable.

6.4. Valuing the Outcomes

An individual making a personal decision can define his preferences through introspection. The policy analyst's task is more complicated. Because one of his primary responsibilities is to help the decision maker define his preference function, a substantial part of this document has been devoted to methods for carrying out this task.

Some valuation problems, particularly those that involve intangibles, do not lend themselves to quantification. In such a case, analysis can address the issue descriptively. Perhaps a proposed welfare program is perceived as damaging the dignity of the recipients; that fact should be included in the analysis as one output of the program, just as the total dollar cost would be. Identifying the key intangibles is as much a part of the analyst's job. In any case, values must be assigned openly and explicitly.

Recognizing that an alternative will inevitably be superior with respect to certain objectives and inferior with respect to others, how should different combinations of valued objectives be compared with one another? Assigning values to specific attributes is only a small part of the difficulty in defining preferences. In almost every serious policy choice, painful tradeoffs must be made among valued attributes. [68]

6.5. Determining a Choice

When all aspects of the analysis are drawn together, what is the preferred course of action? The last step in policy analysis is a most satisfying one, for the sole objective of that analysis has been to make a better decision. Having struggled hard with defining the problem, specifying the objectives, constructing the necessary models, and valuing the alternative outcomes, the policy maker now pulls everything together to make the preferred choice. The situation may be so straightforward he can simply look at the consequences predicted for each alternative and select the one that is best. At the opposite extreme, it may be so complex that he will have to rely on a computer to keep track of what the options are, how the world will behave in response to the possible choices, and what his preferences are among possible outcomes.

One critical lesson is obvious: the purpose of all this work is to help make a better decision. Yet we all know that countless policy studies have led nowhere. Sometimes the fault lies with the public decision makers who don't bother to take advantage of readily accessible information. More often, it is the producers of the analysis who are to blame. Many policy analyses are gathering dust because they are too long or too hard to understand. Remember that the world will never beat a pathway to your door just because you build a better model; analysis is worthless if it can't be communicated to others. The watchword, therefore, is: "Keep it simple." The purpose is to inform the decision maker, not to overwhelm him. Analysis should be presented in such a way that the essential points can be readily grasped and, if necessary, debated.

The choice among competing policy alternatives in never easy, for the future is always uncertain and the inescapable tradeoffs painful. The methods set forth here cannot eliminate these difficulties, but they can help us manage them. By improving our ability to predict the consequences of alternative policies, and providing a framework for valuing those consequences, the techniques of policy analysis lead us toward better decisions.[69]

Unit VII

PUBLIC POLICY AND DEMOCRACY

Economic policies which would tend to reduce regional disparities in a nation is always thought to be desirable. But it is also recognized that attempts to do so may be counterproductive, in the sense that it might lead to distortionary incentives to agents and might have a potential cost in terms of efficiency. In a federal framework, the structure of grant allocation to states have a lot of equity criterion built in them1. However, one needs to examine whether policies designed to ensure equity actually serve the purpose and if they do, the costs that may be associated with it in the form of efficiency. At the same time, one needs to examine political institutions that create incentives to undertake policies that serve to aggravate the already existing regional inequalities. This chapter mainly investigates political structures in a democratic setup which turn out to be discriminatory as well as distortionary and investigates the role of public policy in such a context. The latter half mainly discusses the Indian experience focussing mainly on the redistributive central transfers to states and the efficiency aspects associated with it. We also look at how Indian public policy has been affected by the duration of governments and the nature of representation of states in parliament.

Most electoral systems in democratic countries is characterized by majority rule. This leads to diverse implications under different circumstances. When it comes to the election of a candidate from a particular constituency, the system of election is known as plurality rule, where the candidate getting the largest number of votes wins. This system does not take into account the fact that the selected candidate may be able to win even with a minority of vote share in the case of more than two candidate elections. Moreover this gives weight only to the most preferred candidate of the voter's, so might lead to starkly different electoral results in two candidate and three candidate elections (see **Saari 1999**).

As regards policies taken by government in the light of winning an election, results are more optimistic. **Becker (1983)** argues that special interest groups choose efficient policies to minimize opposition from other groups who pay for the deadweight losses. **Wittman (1989)** reiterates that democratic governments will allocate to the economic markets those tasks in which the economic market is most efficient. Democratic markets need not necessarily be just, but merely aggregate (equally or unequally) the preferences of participants in the political process. People in power resort to efficient policies not out of any altruistic behaviour, but from its own selfish interest to regain power. **Coulingh (1992)** discusses a range of probabilistic voting models where candidates in their quest to maximize expected number of votes implicitly maximize a social welfare function that subsumes all individual interests.

However, it should be noted parties would frame policies to come to power the next term, which may not be possible by maximising the expected number of votes or seats that it wins, but would have the objective of maximizing probability of winning from a majority of seats. This issue was stressed by **Snyder (1989)** in optimal distribution of campaign resources in two party elections, when he pointed out that the two objectives need not be equivalent. The difference is that when parties are concerned about winning a majority of the seats, there is an additional factor that affects the marginal product of spending in a district, namely that the seat is pivotal. The same issue was pointed out by **Seabright (1996),** while discussing that there is a potential cost of centralisation if the central government tries to maximise the probability of winning from a majority of jurisdictions. In such a situation there is a cost of centralisation which is the reduced probability that the welfare of a given region can determine the re-election of the government. This may be seen as a distortion which is brought about by the system of majority voting.

This distortion has important ramifications on the distribution of resources in a democratic system. **Gupta (1998)** examines resource allocation across three jurisdictions when the central government has to win from two of the three jurisdictions.

In the presence of independently distributed electoral uncertainty across jurisdictions, any allocation will help the central government win with certainty if the reservation utility (welfare expected to be provided by the incumbent government to the population) and the electoral uncertainty is very low2.

However, when both reservation utility and electoral uncertainty increase, there comes a point when discrimination is a definite outcome. Resources for local public good are divided between any two of the three jurisdictions. Nevertheless, as both reservation utility and electoral uncertainty increase further, equal allocation of resources between all three jurisdictions comes out as the optimal allocation, which is the same as that of a social planner's. Thus a democratic planner's allocation need not always be distortionary even when the government tries to maximise the probability of winning from a majority of jurisdictions.

However such neat results on discrimination arrived at need not always be possible once we relax the assumption of identical individuals and introduce heterogeneity. With one individual in each jurisdiction and with reservation utility and ability being equal across individuals, it can be shown that the jurisdiction with the individual with the median median weight on local public good gets favoured the most in terms of resource allocation. However, when individuals set their reservation utilities at the level they would expect from a Utilitarian social planner, one cannot say a priori as to which jurisdictions should be favoured. Finally in the case with more than one one individual in each jurisdiction and with heterogenous individuals, problems associated with public goods come up, and here the distribution of population as well as the weights on local public good for the median voter in the jurisdictions becomes important for the allocation problem.

Bardhan and Mukherjee (1998) explicitly discuss the capture of power by local interest groups and their implications in a democratic framework at both the local and national level. Stakes are higher for political parties in central elections than in local elections, resulting in contests that tend to be less skewed on average than are local elections. The number of contesting parties is also typically greater at the central level. National elections tend to be held more frequently and are less prone to booth capturing or strong arm tactics, owing to greater media attention. Moreover, given fixed costs in the formation of lobby groups there may be more lobbies operating at the central level, serving to diffuse the bias secured by any single group. All these factors seem likely to imply that national governments are less prone to capture than local governments.

Although **Bardhan and Mukherjee** explicitly model heterogeneity of voter characteristics in two forms, income status and awareness level of the voters, problems associated with multidimensional voter characteristics do not emerge.

This is because they assume identical demographic profiles across all constituencies. If this is not the case , then the government while maximising its re-election possibilities may tend to target the welfare by more than one particular characteristic in order to satisfy a majority of jurisdictions. If it targets policies for for poor, it satisfies where the poor are in a majority, but the number of these jurisdictions may not be large enough to get it a majority of seats. It then might have to target policies aimed at community A, and then it might win from jurisdictions where community A are in a majority. The government would have to thus ensure that the combined number of poor and community A jurisdictions satisfied, of which some may be overlapping, make up the majority of juridisdictions. The same problem also applies to representatives who form the legislature. Given different dimensions of voter characteristics, legislatures may want to regroup themselves on different issues. The final impact on the voters and resource allocation to jurisdictions is therefore the impact of the multitude of policies that may be taken arising from a multitude of dimensions. It should be noted that the distortion in resource allocation need not necessarily come about only through distortions in the political structure. They may be reinforced by other factors like the tax structure. I consider one such distortion, namely the oversupply of local public goods and the consequent undersupply of central public goods in a federal structure. From a Public Economics angle, **Keen (1998)** explains the possibility of relatively high local tax rates and the consequent oversupply of local public good, even when local governments are benevolent. This happens because both local as well as central government tax the same base, local governments while setting tax rates with the aim of maximizing consumer welfare, taking into account the consumer's valuation of local public good, while ignoring its possible adverse impact on the size of the base and its effect on the provision of central public good, while the central government would consider both. **Buchanan and Tullock (1962)** make a similar point while arguing from teh Public Choice perspective. In their discussion of the simple logrolling model they take up the problem of repair of local roads that lead to the highway. A simple referendum would result in no local road being repaired since the benefits would accrue to a few while the costs would be borne by all. However, a logrolling system would permit local roads to be kept in repair through the emergence of bargains amongst voters and an "equilibrium" would normally tend to involve overinvestment of resources. So to correct such a distortion we would not only need that each government have separate bases for taxation but also institutions that prevent vote trading amongst legislatures.

The literature discussed till now were only static models, where policies of any period did not have any repercussions over time. However if the discriminatory policies of the central government were in the development of infrastructure in certain regions, we can expect the disparity between regions to widen across time going by Myrdal's theory of cumulative causation. By this theory a region with lower growth initially will continue to decline, investment will fall; labour and capital will migrate to high growth regions; with declining availability of skilled labour; growth rate will fall further.

In many cases it might also be difficult to say whether central government policies are discriminatory. Typically in a nation, we might expect some regions to be rich which contribute more to the central pool and thereby expect more infrastructural facilities, while the other regions contribute less and also expect less. A typical example of such a situation might be the residents of a city and a village. Therefore while studying any resource allocation one has to normalise for the effect mentioned. It also need be recognised that in a democratic framework people's expectations depend on what it received from previous governments.

If the government in order to win a election in the present term endows favours to a particular region, the region might expect the same favours to continue and it might become difficult for the government to get elected from the same region unless it does the same3. In such a situation whether a region would get favoured again would depend on whether the increased contribution to the central pool because of its increased activity arising from better infrastructure from last term's favours, is enough to meet its enhanced expectations.

If this be the case then we would expect divergence to grow, if it is not then disparities will not grow over time, although allocation of resources in any time period will be seen to be discriminatory.

Again at this point of time, we should set aside political institutions and examine the question whether balanced regional development is really a feasible alternative for a central government and if such a policy is desirable in the first place. In any country some regions may be endowed with natural resources and may have locational advantages such as being on the coastline which might facilitate its development as ports or trading centres. It may be worthwhile to pursue industrialisation in such areas which automatically leads to a rise in regional disparity. However migration to an extent may reduce the income inequality that may arise out of regional disparity. However, the impact of migration may have a substantial effect in a country like U.S where people are mobile in search of income and employment opportunities, its effect may be limited in a country like India, where people have strong regional identities and if people perceive a definite welfare loss if they do not reside in the region where their community is in a majority. Going by Gordon Tullock's explanation again, majority rule decision making may agree on the development of certain regions if they are accompanied by side payments or redistributive transfers which can then be used for the development of these regions, and the objective of balanced regional growth is somewhat satisfied.

However, redistributive transfers would normally take the form of grants from Central government to the lower levels. Here too there are associated problems. It is normally the case that higher levels of government, namely the central government have less information on tastes and preferences and costs at the local level and would have to rely on local governments for the same. In such a situation local governments would like to overstate costs, not only to corner a part of the resources for the bureaucracy, but also ensure that the jurisdiction bears only a small part of the public expenses, borne within the boundaries. To overcome this problem, **Oates (1972)** suggested that each level of government should try to meet its expenditures from its own resources rather than from external funding. That would mean each level of government must have a sufficiently large tax base and preferably a separate tax base4. Given the fact that tax bases may be limited, and from the efficiency perspective, local governments are assigned tax bases which are immobile (property, etc.) and which are less buoyant (this would mean that tax base does not expand with time), grants in aid therefore become the viable alternative. The Indian Experience Whether economic policies in India have lead to regional inequalities has be a source of debate. As far as the role of transfers are concerned, recent empirical evidence by Ghosh, Marjit and **Neogi (1998)** found that although the allocation of funds across the states have been in accordance with the level of income across the states, growth performances of states do not seem to be converging. They attribute the rising disparity to the lower efficiency with which public capital is utilized particularly in the poorer states and also because of the infrastructural disparity between the states. Jha et. al. (1999) attempt to measure the pure tax efficiency of fifteen major Indian states for the period from 1980/81 to 1992/93 in a manner that allows both efficiency to vary both across time as well as across states. Their results revealed that there exists a moral hazard problem in the design of central grants in the sense that higher grants by central governments to the state governments reduce efficiency of tax collection by these states.

In a study on regional disparities, a study by **Raman (1998),** reveals that recent Finance Commissions (from the sixth commission onwards) have been more equitable and have benefitted poorer states more than richer ones, while the same cannot be said for Planning Commission devolutions. However the type of funding and the share of transfers have changed in the last four commissions, in the sense that the type of automatic transfers have declined. That is finance commission transfers are declining in importance and that the portion of funds which come under the non-statutory type of distribution has increased.

Amongst the poorer states, hill states of Manipur, Meghalaya, Nagaland, Mizoram and Arunachal Pradesh received higher than average level of funding. Among the subsequent finance commissions, the primary aim was to fill nonplan budgetary gaps of states, which are taken to be the financial needs of states. Typically, these estimates are incorrect and leads to further increases in budgetary gaps. The states are able to exploit the non-plan grants in aid, by presenting a set of data that shows the deficits in the states' budget. The nonplan grants are also harmful because the commission attaches no conditionality to the grants, thus, leaving no incentive for the states to improve their deficit situation. Moreover, the rates of return specified by the Finance Commission for state investments are very low and losses still made were covered by the Finance Commissions. Alongside with the Finance Commission, the Planning Commission also disburses funds under the category of Plan expenditures. The funds are provided by the commission on the basis that states would be able to match this amount. This prompts all state governments to provide inflated estimates of expenditure and their revenue. The Planning Commission transfer of resources is done through loans and grants in the ratio 70:30. The high share of loans component means that indebtedness of the states increases in successive plans. At the same time the ratio of grants to loans for the special category states have been in the ratio 90:10, which has meant that these states increasingly rely on central assistance for development expenditures. Plan transfers have been unequal with the special category states getting a much higher resource share than the national average, while other less developed states such as Bihar, Uttar Pradesh and Madhya Pradesh having received a much less share in all Plan periods. Finally the proportion of discretionary transfers which the central government may decide by a formula of its own has risen to about 60% of the total disbursements. **Goerge (1987)** is critical of such transfers and is of the view that such transfers are open to political bargaining and horsetrading.

Till now the discussion had focussed on the problem of central government grant allocation and its impact on equity across states as well as policy distortions that it might induce. It is also at the same time necessary to investigate as to how the duration of democratic governments might lead to distortions in fiscal policies. **Dutta (1996)** tries to explain the same using state election data from 1967 onwards for 15 major states. His main interest was to see the impact on the emergence of short lived coalition governments in the Indian case on their fiscal policies. The main hypothesis being tested is, in a democratic setup, if political power alternates rapidly and randomly between competing parties or groups of parties, then each government will follow myopic policies since it assigns a low probability to being re-elected. Hard policy options whose benefits flow after a long gestation lag are unlikely to be adopted by such a government.

Instead it may spend indiscriminately to satisfy the short term needs of its support groups. This will result in a policy of high debt to its successor. Although this may constrain the next government, the current government does not care of the priorities of the next government. The analysis of data relating to the revenue budgets of major states in India during 1967/68 to 1992/93 does largely seem to support the fact that that unstable ruling coalitions tend to have a significantly higher ratio of revenue expenditure to state domestic product. Problems have also come up from the perspective of political representation of the states in the Lok Sabha. Till 1976, the proportion of seats assigned to a state in the Lok Sabha was in the ratio of the states population to the total population of the country. However, over the years, the southern states have performed very well on the area of population control, while this has not been so for the northern states, as a result in the first few decades after independence, the former were losing out on Lok Sabha seats to the north during the delimitation exercises. To prevent this annomaly, a freeze on Parliamentary seats was done in 1976 for a period of 25 years, which expires in 2001. Given the population projections, a revision based on 2001 cencus would mean U.P gaining 8 seats, Madhya Pradesh 3 and Haryana 1, while Tamil Nadu would loose 6 seats, Kerala 4 and Andhra Pradesh 1. According to demographer Ashish Bose, a skewed distribution of central financial allocations to the states could also result from the expanding population growth differential. While the Central Plan funds will not be affected, distribution of revenue funds such as excise can run into problems. On the other hand continuing with the freeze, and not going in for delimitation would mean over-representation of small constituencies and under-representation of large constituencies especially in urban areas, which is actually against the spirit of the constitution. Apart from the political front, the widening disparities between the north and the south have also had significant economic fallouts. According to Goerge Mathew, southern states being more progressive and stable are attracting more investments and hence offering more job opportunities. In such a situation one cannot rule out the possibility better wages, better living conditions in the south attracting migrants from the north.

CONCLUSION

This chapter gives an insight to motives for discrimination in public policy in a democratic framework, and looks at efficiency arguments on policies designed to ensure equity. In a democratic framework there might be a tendency for central governments to divert resources to a few jurisdictions, given that it has to win by majority rule. However this may not be always so, especially if electoral uncertainty and expectations be high. Such theoretical incentives to discriminate are hard to test empirically, especially when constituencies differ in size, population, income and taste. The concept of balanced regional development may not be also feasible always, especially if regions differ in their natural endowments, a solution to it may be to develop the prospective regions, at the same time go in for redistributive transfers to compensate the economically backward regions. In the case of India, recent Finance Commission devolution have been more equitable, giving a larger proportion to poorer states, while the same cannot be said of the Planning Commission devolution. However what is of concern is the fall in the percentage of statutory transfers in the overall disbursements, and the dramatic rise in the amount disbursed as discretionary transfers which does indicate a political motive. There have also been evidences in India on short lived governments having relatively more revenue expenditure to state domestic product than governments which last its full term, which is an indicator of such governments spending far too much to satisfy interest groups for the sake of immediate electoral gains. Finally we delve into the problem of allocating seats to states in the legislature in such a manner that political power and representation of states is not diluted if they were to implement progressive family planning policies.

Bibliography

BIBLIOGRAPHY

1. Ackoff, Russell L., *Re-creating the Corporation – A Design of Organisations for the 21st Century*, Oxford University Press, New York, 1999

2. Albaek, E. (1998). Knowledge, interests and the many meanings of evaluation: a development perspective. *Scandinavian Journal of Social Welfare, 7*, 94–98.

3. Albaek, E., Christiansen, P.M., and Togeby, L. (2003). Experts in the Mass Media: Researchers as Sources in Danish Daily Newspapers, 1961–2001. *Journalism & Mass Communication,* 80(4), 937–948.

4. Anderson, J.E. (1975). *Public Policymaking.* New York: Praeger.

5. Aguilar, M. *Tratado de Economia.* (Mexico: Aguilar Eds., 1987).

6. Bardhan, Pranab, and Dilip Mukherjee. (1998). "Expenditure decentralization and the delivery of public services in developing countries." Working paper no. C98-104, University of California, Department of Economics, Berkeley, California, U.S.A

7. Becker G. (1983). "A theory of competition among pressure groups for political influence." Quarterly Journal of Economics 98, 371-400. Boadway, Robin, and Michael Keen. (1996). "Efficiency and the optimal direction of federal-state transfers." International Tax and Public Finance 3, 137-155.

8. Boadway, Robin, Isao Horiba and Raghbendra Jha (1998). "Financing and optimal provision of expenditures by government funded decentralized agencies.", ForthcomingPublic Choice.

9. Buchanan, James M. and Gordon Tullock. (1962) The calculus of consent. Ann Arbor: University of Michigan Press.

10. Bachrach, P., and Baratz, M.S. (1962). Two faces of power. American Political Science Review, 56(4), 947–952.

11. Bardach, E. (1976). Policy Termination as a Political Process. Policy Sciences, 7(2), 123–131.

12. Bardach, E. (1977). The Implementation Game: What Happens After a Bill Becomes Law. Cambridge, MA: MIT Press.

13. Baumgartner, F.R., and Jones, B.D. (1993). Agendas and Instability in American Politics. Chicago: University of Chicago Press.

14. Braybrooke, D. *A Strategy of Decision.* (New York: Free Press, 1983).

15. Baumgartner, F.R., and Jones, B.D. (2003). Positive and negative Feedback in Politics. In F.R. Baumgartner and B.D. Jones (eds.), Policy Dynamics, pp. 3–28. Chicago: University of Chicago Press.

16. Behn, R.D. (1978). How to Terminate a Public Policy: A Dozen Hints for the Would-be Terminator. Policy Analysis, 4(3), 393–314.

17. Bovens, M., t'Hart, P., and Peters, G.B. (eds.) (2001). Success and Failure in Public Governance: A Comparative Analysis. Cheltenham: Edward Elgar.

18. Brady, H.E., and Collier, D. (eds.) (2004). Rethinking Social Inquiry. Diverse Tools, Shared Standards. Lanham, MD: Rowman & Littlefi eld.

19. Brewer, G., and deLeon, P. (1983). The Foundations of Policy Analysis. Monterey, Cal.: Brooks, Cole.

20. Burstein, P. (1991). Policy Domains: Organization, Culture, and Policy Outcomes. American Review of Sociology 17: 327–350.

21. Baviskar A. (1995). *In the Belly of the River: Tribal Confl icts over Development in the Tribal Areas.* New Delhi: Oxford University Press.

22. Braibanti, R. (1966). Transnational Inducement of Administrative Reform: A Survey of Scope and Critique of Issues. In J. D. Montgomery and W. J. Siffi n. (eds.), *Approaches to Development: Politics, Administration and Change*. New York: McGraw Hill.

23. Braibanti, R. J., and Spengler, J. J. (eds.), (1963). *Administration and Economic Development in India*. Durham, NC: Duke University Press.

24. Business Today magazine, New Delhi, May 25th 2003 (Also available at http://www.tata.com/tata_sons/media/20030515.htm)

25. Chambers, Robert, *Managing Rural Development*, Scandinavian Institute of African Studies, Uppsala, 1974

26. Commonwealth Secretariat, *Current Good Practices and New Developments in Public Service Management: A Profile of the Public Service of New Zealand*, 1995a

27. Commonwealth Secretariat, *Current Good Practices and New Developments in Public Service Management: A Profile of the Public Service of Malaysia*, 1995b

28. Coughlin, Peter J. (1992). Probabilistic Voting Theory. Cambridge University Press.

29. Coughlin, Peter J., Dennis C. Mueller, and Peter Murrell. (1990). "Electoral politics, interest groups and the size of government." Economic Inquiry 28(4), 682-705.

30. Center for Women's Development Studies (CWDS). (1997). Annual Report CWDS (1996–1997), New Delhi.

31. Cobb, R.W.. Elder, C.D. (1972). Participation in American Politics: The Dynamics of Agenda Building. Boston, MA: Allyn and Bacon.

32. Cobb, R.W., Ross, J.K., and Ross, M.H. (1976). Agenda Building as a Comparative Political Process. American Political Science Review, 70(1), 126–38.

33. Cohen, M.D., March, J., and Olsen, J.P. (1972). A Garbage Can Model of Organizational Choice. Administrative Science Quarterly, 17(1), 1–25.

34. Crenson, M.A. (1971). The Unpolitics of Air Pollution. Baltimore: Johns Hopkins University Press.

35. Correa, H. *Multivariate Analysis*. (Pittsburgh: GSPIA, 1994).

36. deLeon, P. (1978). A Theory of Policy Termination. In J.V. May and A. Wildavsky (eds.), The Policy Cycle, pp. 279-300. Berverly Hills: Sage.

37. deLeon, P. (1999). The Stages Approach to the Policy Process. In P.A. Sabatier (ed.), Theories of the Policy Process, pp. 19–32. Boulder, CO: Westview Press.

38. DeLeon, P., and deLeon, L. (2002). What ever happened to Policy Implementation. An alternative Approach. Journal of Public Administration Research and Theory, 12(4), 467–492.

39. DiMaggio, P.J., and Powell, W.W. (1991). The Iron Cage Revisited: Institutional isomorphism and Collective Rationality in Organization Fields. In W.W. Powell and P.J. DiMaggio (eds.), The New Institutionalism in Organisational Analysis, pp. 63–82. Chicago: Chicago University Press.

40. Döhler, M., and Manow, P. (1995). Strukturbildung von Politikfeldern. Das Beispiel bundesdeutscher Gesundheitspolitik seit den fünfziger Jahren. Opladen: Leske + Budrich.

41. Dogan, M. (1975). The Mandarins of Western Europe. The Political Role of Top Civil Servants. New York: Sage.

42. Dolowitz, D.P., and Marsh, D. (2000). Learning from Abroad: The Role of Policy Transfer in Contemporary Policy-Making. Governance, 13(1), 5–24.

43. Dowding, K. (2003). There Must Be End to Confusion: Policy Networks, Intellectual Fatigue, and the Need for Political Science Methods Courses in British Universities. Political Studies, 49(1), 89–105.

44. Downs, A. (1972). Up and Down with Ecology. The Issue-Attention Cycle. The Public Interest, 28, 38–50.

45. Dunleavy, P.J. (1986). Explaining the Privatization Boom. Public Administration, 64(1), 13–34.

46. Dutta, Bhaskar. (1996) Coalition governments and Fiscal Policies in India IRISIndia Working paper No. 29.

47. Dewey, J. *The Public and Its Problems*. (New York: Holt and Winston Publish., 1987).

48. Dunn, W. *Publlic Policy Analysis*. (New Jersey: Prentice Hall, 1994).

49. D'Souza, D. (2002). *The Narmada Dammed: An Inquiry into the Politics of Development*. New Delhi: Penguin Books.

50. Dahl, R. (1961). *Who Governs?* New Haven, CT: Yale University Press.

51. Dantwala, M.. (1985). Garibi Hatao (Eliminate Poverty) Strategy Options. Economic and Political Weekly, *XX, 11,* 475–476.

52. Dreze, J., Samson, M., and Singh, S. (eds.), (1997). *The Dam and the Nation: Displacement and Resettlement in the Narmada Valley.* New Delhi: Oxford University Press.

53. Darman, Richard, *"Note on Policy Development No. 4"*, cited in Moore,1998.

54. De Merode, L., and Thomas, C.S., "Implementing civil service pay and employment reform in Africa", in Lindauer, David L. and Nunberg, Barbara (eds.), *Rehabilitating Government*, Avebury / Ashgate Publishing Co. Ltd., 1996

55. Economic & Social Commission for Asia & The Pacific, *The Lessons of East / South-East Asian Growth Experience*, Development Paper No. 17, ESCAP, Bangkok, 1995, pp. 92 – 93.

56. Evan, G. and Manning, N., *Helping Governments Keep Their Promises: Making Ministers and Governments More Reliable Through Improved Policy Management,* South Asia Working Paper, World Bank, Washington, 2003.

57. Edelman, M. (1971). Politics as Symbolic Action. Chicago: Markham.

58. Elmore, R.F. (1979/1980). Backward Mapping: Implementation Research and Policy Decisions. Political Science Quarterly, 94, 601–616.

59. Etzioni, A. *The Active Society.* (New York: Free Press, 1989).

60. Eulau, H; Prewitt, K. *Labyrinths of Democracy.* (Indianapolis: Merrill, 1989).

61. Feick, J., and Jann, W. (1988). 'Nations Matter'—aber wie? Vom Eklektizismus zur Integration in der vergleichenden Policy-Forschung. In M.G. Schmidt (ed.), Staatstätigkeit. International und historisch vergleichende Analysen, pp. 196–220. Opladen: Westdeutscher Verlag (Special Issue 19 of Politische Vierteljahresschrift 29).

62. Fischer, F. (1990). Technocracy and the Politics of Expertise. Newbury Park, CA: Sage.

63. Frohok, M. *Public Policy, Scope and Logic.* (New Jersey: Prentice Hall, 1979).

64. Fernandes W. (1995). An Activist Process around the Draft National Rehabilitation Policy. *Social Action, 45, July-Sept.,* 277–298.

65. Fischer, F. (2003). *Reframing Public Policy: Discursive Politics and Deliberative Practices.* Oxford: Oxford University Press.

66. Fischer, F. (1993). Policy Discourse and the Politics of Washington Think Tanks. In F. Fischer and J. Forrester (eds.), *The Argumentative Turn in Policy Analysis and Planning.* Durham and London: Duke University Press, 21–24.

67. Ghosh, Buddhadeb, Sugata Marjit and Chiranjib Neogi. (1998)"Economic growth and regional disparities in India:1960-1995" in Centre for Studies in Social Sciences, Calcutta, Working paper No. 3.

68.   Goerge K. K. (1987). "Discretionary budgetary transfers: A Review"in Centre state budgetary transfers ed Gulati I. S. Oxford University Press.

69.   Gupta Santanu (1998). "Political Accountability and Fiscal Federalism" Presented at Centre for Studies in Social Sciences, in Conference on Regional Diparities: India in the 21st Century, Dec 19, 1998.

70.   Ghosh, J., and Chandrashekhar C.,P. (2002). The Political Economy of the Indian Reform Process. Paper presented at Seminar on The Politics of Economic Reform in India, Centre for Economic and Social Studies, Hyderabad, India. Government of India. (1999). Letter to VHAI. January 8.

71.   Guha, R. (1989). *Unquiet Woods: Ecological Change and Protest in the Himalaya.* New Delhi: Oxford University Press.

72.   Guha, R. (1999). *Savaging The Civilized: Verrier Elwin, His Tribals and India.* New Delhi: Oxford University Press.

73.   Greenberger, M. *Models in Policy Process.* (New York: Russell Found., 1986).

74.   Geva-May, I. (2004). Riding the Wave of Opportunity: Termination in Public Policy. Journal of Public Administration Research and Theory, 14(3), 309–333.

75.   Haas, P.M. (1992). Introduction: Epistemic Communities and International Policy Coordination. International Organization, 42(1), 1–35.

76.   Habermas, J. (1968). Technik und Wissenschaft als Ideologie. Frankfurt, M.: Suhrkamp.

77.   Hargrove, E.C. (1975). The Missing Link: The Study of Implementation of Social Policy. Washington, DC: Urban Institute.

78.   Heclo, H., (1978). Issue networks and the executive establishment. In A. King (ed.), The New American Political System, pp. 87–124.Washington, D.C.: American Enterprise Institute.

79.   Hochman, H. *Redistribution through Public Choice.* (New York: Columbia Univ. Press, 1976).

80.   Heclo, H., and Wildavsky, A. (1974). The Private Government of Public Money: Community and Policy Inside British Politics. London: Macmillan.

81.   Hellstern, G.M., and Wollmann, H. (eds.) (1983). Experimentelle Politik. Reformstrohfeuer oder Lernstrategie. Opladen: Leske + Budrich.

82.   Hill, H.C. (2003). Understanding Implementation: Street-Level Bureaucrats' Resources for Reform. Journal of Public Administration Research and Theory, 13(3): 283–309.

83.   Hill, M., and Hupe, P. (2002). Implementing Public Policy. Governance in Theory and Practice. London: Sage.

84.   Hogwood, B.W., and Gunn, L.A. (1984). Policy-analysis for the real world. Oxford: Oxford University Press.

85.   Hogwood, B., and Peters, G.B. (1983). Policy Dynamics. Brighton: Wheatsheaf.

86.   Hood, C. (1983). The Tools of Government. London: Macmillan.

87.   Hood, C. (1994). Explaining Economic Policy Reversals. Buckingham, Philadelphia: Open University Press.

88.   Hood, C. (2002). The Risk Game and the Blame Game. Government and Opposition, 37(1), 15–37.

89.   Hood, C., Rothstein, H., and Baldwin, R. (2001). The Government of Risk. Understanding Risk Regulation Regimes. Oxford: Oxford University Press.

90.   Howlett, M., and Ramesh, M. (2003). Studying Public Policy. Policy Cycles and Policy Subsystems. 2nd Edition. Oxford: Oxford University Press.

91.   Hajer M. A., and Wagenaar, H. (eds.) (2003). *Deliberative Policy Analysis Understanding Governance in the Network Society* Cambridge: Cambridge University Press.

92.   Hanson, A. H. (1966). *The Process of Planning: A Study of India's Five Year Plans 1950–6.* Oxford: Oxford University Press.

93.   Jha R. et. al. "Tax efficiency in selected Indian states." Empirical Economics forthcoming.

94.   Jayal, N. G. (1997) Consolidating Democracy: Governance and Civil Society in India. Centre for Political Studies, Jawaharlal Nehru University, New Delhi (mimeograph).

95.   Jayal, N. G. (1999) *Democracy and the State Welfare, Secularism and Development in Contemporary India.* New Delhi: Oxford University Press.

96.   Jenkins, R. (1999). *Democratic Politics and Economic Reform in India*. New Delhi: Cambridge University Press.

97.   Jha, A. K. (ed.). (2004). *Women in Panchayati Raj Institutions*. New Delhi, Anmol Publications.

98.   Joshi, A. (1999). Progressive bureaucracy: An oxymoron? The case of Joint Forest Management in India. Paper 24a. Overseas Development Institute, London: Rural Development Forestry Network.

99.   James, O., and Lodge, M. (2003). The Limitations of 'Policy Transfer' and 'Lesson Drawing' for Contemporary Public Policy Research. *Political Studies Review*, 1, 179–193.

100. Jann, W. (2003). State, administration and governance in Germany: competing traditions and dominant narratives. *Public Administration*, 81(1), 95–118.

101. Jann, W. (2004). Einleitung: Instrumente, Resultate und Wirkungen—die deutsche Verwaltung im Modernisierungsschub. In W. Jann, J. Bogumil, G. Bouckaert, D. Budäus, L.

Holtkamp, L. Kißler, S. Kuhlmann, E. Mezger, C. Reichard, and H. Wollmann. *Status-Report Verwaltungsreform. Eine Zwischenbilanz nach zehn Jahren*, pp. 9–21. Berlin: Edition Sigma.

102. Jenkins, W.I., (1978). *Policy-Analysis. A Political and Organisational Perspective.* London: Martin Robertsen.

103. Jones, B.D. (2001). *Politics and the Architecture of Choice. Bounded Rationality and Governance.* Chicago, London: University of Chicago Press.

104. Jones, Ch. *The Study of Public Policy.* (Monterrey: Brooks, 1990).

105. Kaufman, H. (1976). *Are Government Organizations Immortal?* Washington, DC: Brookings.

106. Kalshian, Rakesh. (1999)"Fertility is power: mother of all paradoxes" Outlook March 8, 24-26.

107. Keen Michael (1998). "Vertical tax externalities in the theory of fiscal federalism" IMF Staff Papers 45(3), 454-485.

108. Kenis, P., and Schneider, V. (1991). Policy Networks and Policy Analysis: Scrutinizing an new analytical toolbox. In B. Marin and R. Mayntz (eds), *Policy Networks. Empirical Evidence and Theoretical Considerations*, pp. 25–59. Frankfurt and Boulder, CO: Campus and Westview Press.

109. Kingdon, J.W. (1995). *Agenda, Alternatives, and Public Policies.* 2nd Edition. New York: HarperCollins College Publishers.

110. Kuhn, T.S. (1962). *The Structure of Scientifi c Revolutions.* Chicago: University of Chicago Press.

111. Khan, A. M. (1997). *Shaping Policy: Do NGOs Matter? Lessons from India.* New Delhi: Society for Participatory Research in Asia.

112. Kohli, A. (1989). Politics of Economic Liberalization in India. *World Development, 17, 3*, 305–328.

113. Kothari, R. (1970). *Politics in India.* Boston: Little and Brown.

114. Krueger, A. O. (1974). The Political Economy of the Rent-Seeking Society. *American Economic Review* 64, 3: 291–303.

115. Kliksberg, Bernardo, "Unconventional Theses about Participation", *International Review of Administrative Sciences*, Vol. 66 No. 1, March 2000

116. Klitgaard, Robert, "Integrating Public Services – a framework for policy analysis", pp. 158 – 9 in *Adjusting to Reality – Beyond State versus Market in Economic Development*, International Centre for Economic Growth, San Francisco, 1991.

117. Lindblom, Charles E., Inquiry and Change: The Troubled Attempt to Understand and Shape Society, Yale University Press, New Haven, 1990.

118. Lasswell, H. *A Preview of Policy Sciences.* (New York: Elsevier, 1992).

119. Lasswell, H.D. (1956). The Decision Process: Seven Categories of Functional Analysis. College Park: University of Maryland Press.

120. Lehmbruch, G. (1991). The organization of society, administrative strategies, and policy networks: Elements of a developmental theory of interest systems. In R. Czada and A. Windhoff-Héritier (eds.), Political Choice: Institutions, Rules, and the Limits of Rationality, pp. 121–158. Frankfurt, M. and Boulder, Col: Campus and Westview Press.

121. Levine, R.A., Salomon, M.A., Hellstern, G.M., and Wollmann, H. (eds.) (1981). Evaluation Research and Practice: Comparative and International Perspectives. Beverly Hills, London: Sage.

122. Lin, A.C. (2000). Reform in the Making. The Implementation of Social Policy in Prison. Princeton, NJ: Princeton University Press.

123. Lindblom C.E. (1959). The Science of Muddling Through. Public Administration Review, 19(2), 79–88.

124. Lindblom C.E. (1968). The Policy-Making Process. Englewood Cliffs, N.J.: Prentice Hall, (1st ed.).

125. Lindblom C.E. (1979): Still Muddling, Not yet Through. Public Administration Review, 39(6), 517–526.

126. Lindblom, C.E., and Cohen, D.K. (1979). Usable Knowledge. Social Science and Social Problem Solving. New Haven, London: Yale University Press.

127. Lipsky, M. (1980). *Street-Level Bureaucracy: Dilemmas of the Individual in Public Services*. New York: Russell Sage Foundation.

128. Lodge, M., and Hood, C. (2002). Pavlovian Policy Responses to Media Feeding Frenzies? Dangerous Dogs Regulation in Comparative Perspective. *Journal of Contingencies and Crisis Management*, 10(1), 1–13.

129. Lodge, M. (2003). Institutional Choice and Policy Transfer: Reforming British and German Railway Regulation. *Governance*, 16(2), 150–178.

130. Lodge, M., and Wegrich, K. (2005a). Governing Multi-Level Governance: Comparing Domain Dynamics in German Land-local Relationships and Prisons. *Public Administration*, 88(2).

131. Lodge, M., and Wegrich, K. (2005b). Control over Government: Institutional Isomorphism and Governance Dynamics in German Public Administration. *Policy Studies Journal*, 33(2), 213–234.

132. Lynn, Lawrence E., Knowledge and Power – The Uncertain Connection, National Academy of Sciences, Washington DC, 1978.

133. Lynn, Lawrence E., "Policy Analysis in the Bureaucracy: How New? How Effective?", Journal of Policy Analysis and Management, Vol. 8, No. 3, 1989.

134. Moore, Mark H., Creating Public Value – Strategic Management in Government, Harvard University Press, Cambridge, 1998.

135. Marin, B. (1990). Generalized Political Exchange. Preliminary Considerations. In B. Marin (ed.), *Generalized Policy Exchange*, pp. 27–66. Boulder, CO: Westview Press.

136. Marin, B., and Mayntz, R. (eds) (1991): *Policy Networks. Empirical Evidence and Theoretical Considerations.* Frankfurt, M./Boulder, CO: Campus and Westview.

137. May, P.J. (1991). Reconsidering policy design: policies and publics. *Journal of Public Policy*, 11(2), 187– 206.

138. May, J.P., and Wildavsky, A. (ed.) (1978). *The Policy Cycle.* Beverly Hills, CA: Sage.

139. Mayntz, R. (1979). Public Bureaucracies and Policy Implementation. *International Social Science Journal*, 31(4), 633–645.

140. Mayntz, R. (ed) (1983). Einleitung: Probleme der Theoriebildung in der Implementationsforschung. In R. Mayntz (ed), *Implementation politischer Programme II. Ansätze zur Theoriebildung*, pp. 7–24. Opladen: Westdeutscher Verlag.

141. Mayntz, R., and Scharpf, F.W. (1975). *Policy-Making in the German Federal Bureaucracy.* Amsterdam: Elsevier.

142. Mayntz, R., and Scharpf, F.W. (1995). Der Ansatz des akteurzentrierten Institutionalismus. In R. Mayntz and F.W. Scharpf (eds.), *Gesellschaftliche Selbstregulierung und politische Steuerung*, pp. 39–71. Frankfurt and New York: Campus.

143. March, J. G., and Olsen, J. P. (1989) *Rediscovering Institutions: The Organizational Basis of Politics.* New York: The Free Press.

144. Mathur, K. (2001). Governance and Alternative Sources of Policy Advice: The Case of India. In K. Weaver and P.B. Stares (eds.), *Guidance for Governance. Comparing Alternative Sources of Public Advice*, pp. 207–230. Tokyo and Washington, D.C.: Japan Centre for International Exchange and Brookings Institute.

145. Mathur, K., and Jayal, N. G. (1992). *Drought Policy and Politics: The Need for a Long Term Perspective.* New Delhi: Sage Publications.

146. Mathur, K., and Bjorkman, J.W. (1994). *Top Policy Makers in India Cabinet Ministers and Civil Service Advisors.* Delhi: Concept Publishers.

147. Musgrave Richard .A (1983). "Who should tax, where and what?" in Tax assignment in Federal Countries ed McLure C.E, 2-19, ANU Press Canberra, Australia.

148. Nanda, N. (1999). *Forests for Whom? Destruction & Restoration in the U.P. Himalayas.* New Delhi: Har-Anand Publications.

149. Nakurama, R., (1987). The Textbook Process and Policy Implementation Research. *Policy Studies Review*, 1, 142–154.

150. Nagel, S. *Enclycopedia of Policy Studies.* (New York: Marcel Dekker, 1991).

151. Oates, Wallace E. (1972). Fiscal Federalism, New York: McGraw-Hill.

152. Ochaeta R. *Procesos de Politica Publlica.* (Guatemala: INAP, 1993).

153. Olson, M. *The Logic of Collective Action.* (Cambridge: Harvard University Press, 1991).

154. Orellana, E. *Introduccion y Aplicaciones de la Teoria de Caos.* (Mexico: LIMUSA, 1989).

155. O'Toole, L.J. (2000). Research on Policy Implementation. Assessment and Prospects. *Journal of Public Administration Research and Theory*, 19(2), 263–288.

156. OECD (2002). *Regulatory Policies in OECD Countries. From Interventionism to Regulatory Governance.* Paris: OECD.

157. Olsen, J.P. (1991). Political Science and Organisation Theory: Parallel Agendas but Mutual Disregard. In R. Czada and A. Windhoff-Héritier (eds.), *Political Choice. Institutions, Rules, and the Limits of Rationality*, pp. 887–119. Frankfurt, M. and Boulder, CO: Campus and Westview Press.

158. Office of the Civil Service Commission, *Compendium of ASEAN Civil Service Systems*, Bangkok, 1997

159. Porter, Roger, *and Presidential Decision Making*: The Economic Policy Board, Cambridge University Press, Cambridge, 1980.

160. Parsons, W. (1995). *Public Policy. An introduction to the Theory and Practice of Policy Analysis*. Aldershot: Edward Elgar.

161. Pollitt, C. (2003). *The Essential Public Manager*. Maidenhead and Philadelphia: Open University Press/Mc- Graw Hill.

162. Pressman, J.L., and Wildavsky, A. (1984). *Implementation. How great expectations in Washington are dashed in Oakland*. (1st ed. 1973), Berkeley: University of California Press.

163. Prittwitz, V. v. (1993). Katastrophenparadox und Handlungskapazität. Theoretische Orientierungen der Politikanalyse. In A. Héritier (eds.), *Policy-Analyse. Kritik und Neuorientierung*, pp. 328–355. Opladen: Westdeutscher Verlag.

164. Pierre, J. (ed.). (2000). *Debating Governance: Authority, Steering, and Democracy*. Oxford: Oxford University Press.

165. Rath, N. (1985). Garib Hatao (Eliminate Poverty): Can IRDP do it? *Economic and Political Weekly, 20, 6,* 238–246.

166. Roy, A., Dey, N., and Singh, S. (2001). Demanding Accountability. *Seminar, 500, 2.*

167. Raymond A. *Study of Policy Formation.* (New York: Free Press, 1992).

168. Raymond, A. *Public Policy Process*. (New York: Free Press, 1988).

169. *Report of the 5th Pay Commission*, Government of India, 1996.

170. Rothenberg, J. *The Measurement of Social Welfare*. (New Jersey: Prentice-Hall, 1982).

171. Russell L. Ackoff and Maurice W. Sasieni, *Fundamentals of Operations Research* (New York:Wiley, 1968).

172. Richardson, J.J., Gustafsson, G., and Jordan, G. (1982). The concept of policy style. In J.J. Richardson. (ed), *Policy styles in Western Europe*, pp. 1–16. London: Allen & Unwin.

173. Raman Jaishankar. (1998). Regional disparities in India unpublished Ph.D thesis, Notterdame University.

174. Saari, Donald G. and Maria M. Tataru. (1999). "The likelihood of dubious election outcomes" Economic Theory Vol 13, 345-363.

175. Sabatier, P.A. (1991). Toward Better Theories of the Policy Process. *Political Science and Politics*, 24, 147–156.

176. Samayoa A. *Aplicaciones del Analisis de Costo-Beneficio*. (Guatemala, USAC, 1987).

177. Samuelson, P. *Economics*. (Boston: MIT, 1993).

178. Schultze, Ch. *The Public Use of Private Interest*. (Washington, D.C.: The Brookings Institution, 1992).

179. Smith, D. *Pragmatism and the Group Theory of Politics.* (New York: BCB, 1988).

180. Stokey, E. *A Primer for Public Policy.* (London: Norton, 1991).

181. Sabatier, P.A. (1993). Advocacy-Koalitionen, Policy-Wandel und Policy-Lernen: Eine Alternative zur Phasenheuristik. In A. Héritier (ed.), Policy-Analyse. Kritik und Neuorientierung (Special Issue 24 of Politische Vierteljahresschrift 34), pp. 116–148 Opladen: Westdeutscher Verlag.

182. Sabatier, P.A., (1999): The Need for Better Theories. In P.A. Sabatier (ed.), Theories of the Policy Process, pp. 3–17. Boulder, CO: Westview.

183. Sabatier, P.A., and Jenkins-Smith, H. (eds.) (1993). Policy change and learning: an advocacy coalition approach. Boulder, CO: Westview.

184. Salamon, L.M. (ed.) (2002). The Tools of Government. A Guide to the new Governance, Oxford: Oxford University Press.

185. Scharpf, F.W. (1973). Verwaltungswissenschaft als Teil der Politikwissenschaft. In F.W. Scharpf, Planung als politischer Prozeß: Aufsätze zur Theorie der planenden Demokratie, pp. 3–32. Frankfurt: Suhrkamp.

186. Schattschneider, E.E. (1960). The Semi-Sovereign People. New York: Holt, Rinehart and Winston.

187. Schlager, E. (1999). A Comparison of Frameworks, Theories, and Models of Policy Processes. In P.A. Sabatier (ed.), Theories of the Policy Process, pp. 233–260. Boulder, CO: Westview.

188. Schmitter, P.C., and Lehmbruch, G. (eds.) (1979): Trends toward Corporatist Intermediation. London: Sage.

189. Sieber, S. (1981). Fatal Remedies. The Ironies of Social Intervention. New York, London: Plenum Press.

190. Simon, H.A. (1947). Administrative Behavior. A Study of decision-making Processes in administrative Organizations. New York: Macmillan.

191. Stone, D. (2001). Policy Paradox. The Art of Political Decision Making. Revised Edition. New York: Norton.

192. Stone, D. (2004). Transfer Agents and Global Networks in the 'Transnationalisation' of Policy. Journal of European Public Policy, 11(3), 545–66.

193. Seabright, Paul. (1996). "Accountability and decentralization in government: An incomplete contracts model" European Economic Review Vol 40, 61-89.

194. Snyder, James M. (1989). "Election goals and the allocation of campaign resources." Econometrica 57(3), 637-660.

195. Tobin, J. *Introduccion a las Ecuaciones Diferenciales*. (Bogota: McGraw-Hill, 1990).

196. Torres-Rivas Edelberto. *Interpretacion del Desarrollo Social Centroamericano*. (San Jose: EDUCA, 1988).

197. Truman, D. *The Govermental Process* (New York: Knopf, 1992).

198. Taylor, C. C., Ensminger, D., Johnson, H.W.U., and Joyce, J. (1966). India's Roots of Democracy: A Sociological Analysis of Rural India's Experience in Planned Development Since Independence. Bombay: Orient Longmans.

199. Times of India. (1999). Letter to VHAI. January 18.

200. Varshney, A. (1995). Democracy Development and the Countryside Urban Rural struggles in India. Cambridge: Cambridge University Press.

201. Varshney, A. (1999). Mass politics or Elite Politics: India's Economic Reforms in Comparative Perspective. In J. D. Sachs, A. Varshney and N. Bajpai (eds.), India in the Era of Economic Reforms, pp. 222–260. New Delhi: Oxford University Press.

202. Vyasalu, P., and Vyasalu, V. (2000). Women in the Panchayati Raj: Grassroots Democracy in India. Proceedings of Women's Political Participation and Good Governance: 21st Century Challenges, pp. 41–48. New Delhi: UNDP.

203. Vedung, E. (1998). Policy Instruments: Typologies and Theories. In M.-L. Bemelmans-Videc, R.C. Rist, and E. Vedung (eds.), *Carrots, Sticks & Sermons. Policy Instruments & Their Evaluation*, pp. 21–58. New Brunswick and London: Transaction Publishers.

204. Wittrock, B., Wagner, P., and Wollmann, H. (1991). Social science and the modern state: policy knowledge and political institutions in Western Europe and the United States. In P.

Wagner, C.H. Weiss, B. Wittrock and H. Wollmann (eds.), *Social Sciences and Modern States*, pp. 28–85. Cambridge: Cambridge University Press.

205. Weiss, C.H. (1972). *Evaluating Action Programs.* Boston: Allyn & Bacon.

206. Weiss, C.H. (ed.) (1977). *Using Social Research in Public Policy Making.* Lexington, MA: Lexington Books.

207. Weiss, C.H. (1992). *Organizations for Policy Analysis: Helping Government Think.* Newbury Park, CA: Sage.

208. Wittrock, B. (1991). Social knowledge and public policy: eight models of interaction. In P. Wagner, C.H. Weiss, B. Wittrock, and H. Wollmann (eds.), *Social Sciences and Modern States*, pp. 333–353. Cambridge: Cambridge University Press.

209. Wholey, J.S. (1983). *Evaluation and effective Public Management.* Boston, MA: Little Brown.

210. Wildavsky, A. (1964). *The Politics of the Budgetary Process.* Boston, MA: Little Brown.

211. Wildavsky, A. (1969). Rescuing Policy Analysis for PPBS. *Public Administration Review*, 29(2), 189–202.

212. Wildavsky, A. (1972). The Self-Evaluating Organization. *Public Administration Review*, 32(5), 509–520.

213. Wildavsky, A. (1979). *Speaking Truth to Power. The Art and Craft of Policy Analysis.* Boston, MA: Little Brown.

214. Wildavsky, A. (1988). *The New Politics of the Budgetary Process.* Glenview, Illinois and Boston, MA: Scott Foresman/Little Brown.

215. Wollmann, H. (1984). Policy Analysis. Some Observations on the West German Scene. *Policy Sciences*, 17, 27–47.

216. Weber, M. *Economia y Sociedad.* (Mexico: Fondo de Cultura Economica, 1991)

217. Wright, M. *The Power Elite.* (New York: Oxford University Press, 1989)

NOTES

1. See Weber, M. *Economia y Sociedad.* (Mexico: Fondo de Cultura Economica, 1991). p. 12-34.

2. See Torres-Rivas Edelberto. *Interpretacion Del Desarrollo Social Centroamericano.* (San Jose: EDUCA, 1988). p. 35-42.

3. Raymond A. *Study of Policy Formation.* (New York: Free Press, 1992). p. 15-23.

4. Ibid. p. 25.

5. Dewey, J. *The Public and Its Problems.* (New York: Holt and Winston Publish., 1987) p. 17.

6. Smith, D. *Pragmatism and the Group Theory of Politics.* (New York: BCB, 1988). p. 32.

7. Samuelson, P. *Economics.* (Boston: MIT, 1993), p. 23-25; 45-53.

8.   Hochman, H. *Redistribution through Public Choice.* (New York: Columbia University Press, 1976). p. 34-36.

9.   Ibid. p. 44.

10.   Stokey, E. *A Primer for Public Policy.* (London: Norton, 1991). p. 12.

11.   Jones, Ch. *The Study of Public Policy.* (Monterrey: Brooks, 1990). p.17-19

12.   Ibid. p. 21

13.   Ibid. p. 43.

14.   Nagel, S. *Enclycopedia of Policy Studies.* (New York: Marcel Dekker, 1991) . p. 55.

15.   Jones, Ch. Ob.Cit. p. 54.

16.   Lasswell, H. *A Preview of Policy Sciences.* (New York: Elsevier, 1992), p. 54-58.

17.   Truman, D. *The Govermental Process* (New York: Knopf, 1992), p. 66.

18.   Ibid.

19.   Ochaeta R. *Procesos de Politica Publlica.* (Guatemala: Instituto Nacional de Administracion Publica, 1993), p. 45-48.

20.   Wright, M. *The Power Elite.* (New York: Oxford University Press, 1989)

21.   Ochaeta R. Ob. Cit. p. 71

22.   Eulau, H; Prewitt, K. *Labyrinths of Democracy.* (Indianapolis: Merrill, 1989). p. 41.

23.   Ibid.

24.   Ibid. p. 473.

25.   Stokey, E. Ob. Cit. 11.

26.   Jones, Ch. Ob. Cit. p. 30-33.

27.   Dunn, W. *Publlic Policy Analysis.* (New Jersey: Prentice Hall, 1994). p. 226.

28.   Ibid.

29.   Frohok, M. *Public Policy, Scope and Logic.* (New Jersey: Prentice Hall, 1979). p. 45.

30.   Jones, Ch. Ob.Cit. p. 30-31.

31.   Ibid. p. 31.

32.   Etzioni, A. *The Active Society.* (New York: Free Press, 1989). Chapter 12.

33.   Braybrooke, D. *A Strategy of Decision.* (New York: Free Press, 1983). p. 77-85

34.   Ibid.

35.   Ibid. p. 87.

36.   See Raymond, B. *The Study of Policy Formation.* (New York: Free Press, 1988).

37.   Stokey, E. Ob. Cit. p. 26-28.

38.   Ibid. p. 31.

39.   Olson, M. *The Logic of Collective Action.* (Cambridge: Harvard University Press, 1991). p.55.

40.   Stokey E. Ob. Cit. p. 36.

41.   Ibid.p.38.

42.   Correa, H. *Multivariate Analysis.* (Pittsburgh: GSPIA, 1994). p. 18-23.

43.   Stokey, E. Ob.Cit.p. 48-49.

44.   Ibid. p. 50.

45.   Schultze, Ch. *The Public Use of Private Interest.* (Washington, D.C.: The Brookings Institution, 1992). p.33.

46.   Ibid. p. 42.

47.   Tobin, J. *Introduccion a las Ecuaciones Diferenciales.* (Bogota: McGraw-Hill, 1990). p. 23-34.

48.   Stankey, E. Ob.Cit. p. 76.

49.   Ibid. 80-81.

50.   See for example, Russell L. Ackoff and Maurice W. Sasieni, *Fundamentals of Operations Research* (New York: Wiley, 1968).

51.   Orellana, E. *Introduccion y Aplicaciones de la Teoria de Caos.* (Mexico: LIMUSA, 1989). P.18-24.

52.   Ibid. p. 33.

53.   Aguilar, M. *Tratado de Economia.* (Mexico: Aguilar Eds., 1987).p.57.

54.   Stokey, E. Ob.Cit.p.97.

55.   Ibid.p.98.

56.   Ibid.

57.   Ibid. p. 101.

58.   Ibid.p. 104-105; Orellana, E. Ob.Cit. p. 65; and Tobin, J. Ob.Cit.p.88.

59.   Stakey, E. Ob.Cit. p.107.

60.   Greenberger, M. *Models in Policy Process.* (New York: Russell Found., 1986).

61.   Stakey, E. Ob. Cit. p.156.

62.   Samayoa A. *Aplicaciones del Analisis de Costo-Beneficio.* (Guatemala, USAC, 1987).p.43-47

63.   Stakey, E. Ob.Cit. p.154.

64.   Ibid. p. 156.

65.   Jones, Ch. Ob.Cit. p. 233-238; Stakey, E. Ob.Cit. p.321.

66.   Jones, Ch. Ob.Cit. p. 239.

67.   Stakey, Ob.Cit. p.324.

68.   Ibid, p. 325; and Rothenberg, J. *The Measurement of Social Welfare.* (New Jersey: Prentice-Hall, 1982).p.56.

69.   Stakey, Ob.Cit. p.327-329.